WHAT IS MY CAT REALLY THINKING?

for all your gift books and gift stationery

This edition first published in Great Britain in 2023
by Allsorted Ltd, UK WD19 4BG

© Susanna Geoghegan Gift Publishing

Author: Michael Powell
Editor: Sasha Morton

Photographs under licence from Shutterstock.com

Cover and concept design: Milestone Creative
Contents design: seagulls .net

ISBN: 9781912295906

Printed in China

10 9 8 7 6 5 4 3 2 1

"If a cat spoke, it would say things like 'Hey, I don't see the problem here'."

ROY BLOUNT JR.

CONTENTS

INTRODUCTION

Cats, those cute, agile, independent, inscrutable, graceful creatures that share our lives. They sure are puzzling. One moment, they appear to possess a depth of complexity that eludes our understanding; the next moment it dawns on you that they know they can get whatever they want just by miaowing loudly.

Have you ever found yourself slowly blinking at your cat, wondering what mysteries lie behind those enigmatic eyes?

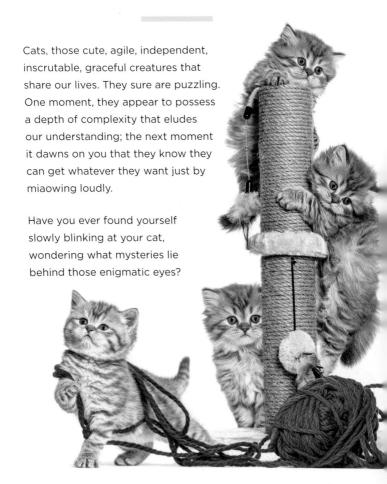

If so, you're not alone. Welcome to the absorbing world of feline cognition, where we embark on a quest to unravel the enigma of our beloved companions.

This book is an exploration of the feline psyche, peering into the depths of their thoughts, emotions and desires. It will help you to understand the inner workings of these mysterious creatures and shed light on many of their often-baffling behaviours.

With a blend of scientific research, expert advice and a reader-friendly format, we strive to bridge the communication gap between humans and cats, to decipher the meaning behind their meows and other vocalizations and interpret their often highly nuanced body language.

By understanding what truly goes on inside those tiny heads, you can forge a stronger bond with your furry companions. You will gain a deeper appreciation for their perspectives and forever change the way you see your unique feline friends, ensuring they are healthy, happy, and above all, able to express their true selves.

WELCOME
HOME

CATS CAN GREET THEIR OWNERS IN DIFFERENT
WAYS WHEN THEY COME HOME, DEPENDING ON THEIR
PERSONALITY AND THE RELATIONSHIP. SOME CATS
RUN TO THE DOOR AND MEOW, TRILL AND PURR, OR
RUB AGAINST THEIR OWNER'S ANKLES. SOME PLACE
THEIR FRONT PAWS UP THE OWNER'S LEGS TO GET
CLOSER TO THEIR FACE (CATS GREET EACH OTHER
BY TOUCHING AND SMELLING NOSE TO NOSE).
OTHER CATS MAY COOLLY OBSERVE THEIR
OWNER'S ARRIVAL FROM A DISTANCE.

If your cat is an active greeter, you may notice that her tail is held vertically. Cats use this friendly tail greeting on humans and other cats. If her tail is up and quivering, it means she's really pleased to see you; but if her tail is hooked at the end, her friendliness is mixed with some uncertainty (maybe you have noisy shopping bags or are with a strange visitor).

However, even sociable cats prefer calm and quiet greetings. Excessive noise and excitement can be a real turn-off and may even be the reason why your cat greets you from afar with a raised tail and a casual meow or two. Regardless, it's always best to approach gently and in a relaxed way.

Whether your cat comes to greet you or simply pops her tail in the air as she passes by, you must acknowledge her and respond to her greeting. By giving her your full attention and actively returning the greeting both verbally and physically, you can build a stronger bond of trust.

These interactions are also crucial for reinforcing the sense of belonging within your household, as each greeting reaffirms your cat's membership in the group. Taking the time to fully engage in these moments can deepen the bond between you and your feline companion. Show your cat some affection by gently rubbing her neck or crouching down to her level so that she can see your face and rub her scent onto you.

> 'I love cats because I enjoy my home; and little by little, they become its visible soul.'
>
> Jean Cocteau

Rubbing is an integral part of the greeting. Cats have specialized scent glands beneath their chins, at the corners of their mouths, on either side of their forehead, at the base of their tails and between their toes. These glands secrete a detailed chemical marker that conveys important information such as social status, territorial boundaries and even sexual availability. Cats greet each other by rubbing against one another to share and exchange these scent markers.

Although cats are known to mark their signature scent on various objects in the house, including furniture, door frames, curtains, humans, discarded clothing and other animals, they tend to prioritize specific areas that they will revisit repeatedly. These areas may include entrances to the home, nesting places, areas with high animal traffic and territorial boundaries. Scent marking in these areas can help prevent physical fights over territory, which are always a last resort.

As a cat owner, it's important to remember that both you and your home are covered with cat pheromones – the equivalent of your cat's lengthy Tinder profile. While it may be tempting to interpret your cat's rubbing behaviour as a form of ownership or possession, this is not entirely accurate. She is

spreading
her scent
as well as
collecting scents
from others, which
helps to strengthen
the sense of belonging
and communal
ownership within the
household. By mingling
their scents, cats not
only show affection but
promote a collective
sense of ownership
and love.

Some cats may also
show affection by
jumping onto their
owner's lap or seeking
attention through
playful behaviour, such
as chasing toys or requesting to be
petted. Some cats bring small gifts, such as toys or leaves
to show their appreciation for their owner's return. She may
even exhibit a unique behaviour to further engage your
attention if she is feeling content. This will vary depending
on the individual cat, but one example could be her pressing
down on your foot with her back paw and repeating the

action a few times – a gesture that can be seen as a form of feline hug. It's important to be aware of these idiosyncrasies as they will differ from cat to cat. Cats don't gesture accidentally, and all physical contact is loaded with meaning.

Not all cats are naturally affectionate or outgoing, and some may take time to warm up to their owners or prefer to greet them in their own unique ways. Overall, each cat has its own individual personality and preferences, so it's essential to understand and respect your cat's behaviour and body language to build a strong and loving bond.

Your greeting is important. A brief or dismissive 'Hi,' followed by annoyed grunts as your cat weaves between your legs is insufficient and rude. Cats are masters at this type of ritualistic behaviour, and we could benefit from learning from them. You should greet all members of your household with full presence and attention, just as our feline friends do. Often, we may shout a greeting while rushing upstairs or mumble to one another as we collapse on the sofa. By taking cues from our cats and sharing in the courtesy of meaningful greetings, we can strengthen the bonds within our entire family unit.

'If a dog jumps into your lap, it is because he is fond of you; but if a cat does the same thing, it is because your lap is warmer.'

Alfred North Whitehead

I'M 'TRILLED' TO SEE
YOU

THE PHYSICAL GREETING GESTURES OF CATS,
WHICH INCLUDE AN UPRIGHT TAIL, CONFIDENT STRIDES
AND LOOKING AT YOUR FACE, ARE TYPICALLY – BUT
NOT ALWAYS – ACCOMPANIED BY WELCOMING SOUNDS.
THE TRILL OF A CAT'S WELCOME IS OFTEN DESCRIBED
AS A MIX OF A MEOW AND A PURR – 'MRRRP!'.
TRILLING IS OFTEN USED BETWEEN ADULT CATS AS
AN EXPRESSION OF AFFECTION AND HAPPINESS.

13

However, not all cats do this, so don't be sad if your cat isn't a triller, because she will have her own unique way of showing her love. Cats with lively and outgoing personalities are more likely to trill, while those who are shy may be less inclined to use this vocalization as a way of expressing their emotions.

When one cat greets another with a trill, it's common to hear an acknowledgement sound in response, typically a short, inhaled purr that is falling in pitch. Trilling is generally a positive high-pitched noise produced with the mouth closed and only lasts for a second or so. If you want to try it out yourself, experiment by making this sound when you return home or matching trill for trill, and you might even spark a bit of conversation with your cat.

You may be curious why your cat prefers to trill instead of simply meowing to say 'Hello'. That's because cats have a range of over 100 vocalizations that genuinely signify different things and are appropriate for different situations. Besides greeting with trills, your cat might also use trilling to grab your attention and direct it towards something interesting, such as an empty food bowl or to beg for treats.

'If your cat continues to look at you, whilst moving away and trilling, she may be asking you to follow her. Sometimes cats will use trilling as a way to get your attention so they can show you something.'

Sara Nelms, pet expert

The greeting trill is comparable to the rolled meow that a mother cat uses to summon her kittens or to approach another cat in a friendly manner. When the mother cat arrives with prey, she makes a gargling sound that varies depending on the type of prey caught. This may be because different prey species pose different degrees of risk; for instance, an injured rat may be more dangerous than a bird or mouse.

If your cat is older or entering their senior years, pay closer attention to her trilling, as it may be a sign of a more serious issue.

'In some instances, an increase in your cat's trilling or even sudden, excessive trilling can be a sign that your cat is in pain, is injured or even unwell . . . If you're not sure whether or not to be concerned, take your cat to the vet.'

Paul Martinez, veterinarian

PLAY
WITH ME

WHEN CATS WANT TO PLAY, THEY OFTEN
COMMUNICATE THEIR DESIRE THROUGH VARIOUS
BODY LANGUAGE ACTIONS AND NOISES. SOME
TYPICAL WAYS THEY SIGNAL THEIR INTEREST IN PLAY
INCLUDE POUNCING, TAIL AND EAR MOVEMENTS,
VOCALIZATIONS, RUBBING AGAINST OBJECTS
AND COLLECTING TOYS.

Not all cats use the same signals to invite play, and some may be more reserved than others.

The invitation to play isn't always as obvious as bringing a toy, dropping it at your feet and looking up expectantly, although cats do of course do this. If you always respond to this behaviour by playing with your cat, then he will quickly appreciate that he has trained you to respond accordingly, so he may not ever have to resort to less obvious cues.

Another common way that cats invite play is by pouncing. Your cat crouches down and then leaps forward, either onto a toy or towards your hand or foot. Whilst it's acceptable for your cat to invite play by mock-attacking you, you should quickly transfer his attention to a toy, because you don't want to teach him that hunting you is acceptable behaviour. It's very cute to have your extremities stalked and nibbled by a kitten, but it's irritating and dangerous to encourage this into your cat's adulthood. Imagine not being able to walk around your house without your cat leaping out from behind a curtain or pouncing on you from the top of a kitchen cabinet. That's an extreme situation, but that is your future unless you discourage it early on.

Likewise, if you invite your kitten to play by wiggling your toes under the duvet, he may grow up to relentlessly pounce on any movement under the duvet, which can become frustrating. It's better to avoid teaching this behaviour altogether, rather than trying to unlearn it later. Avoid taunting games in general, as they can easily descend into bullying, which will undermine your kitten's confidence.

> 'Kittens will use a "Play Face" to indicate their friendly intentions ... they may also use special movements of their tails to signal playfulness, but so far no scientist has been able to decode these.'
>
> John Bradshaw, *Cat Sense*

Cats rub against furniture or other objects to mark their territory, and sometimes as a displacement activity when they are feeling anxious or out of sorts, but it can also indicate a playful mood. Respect your cat's boundaries and don't push him to play if he doesn't want to. Other clues to his playful mood are his tail and ear movements. Cats may twitch their tails or flick their ears back and forth as a sign of excitement and readiness to play.

Jackson Galaxy's book, *Total Cat Mojo*, introduces the acronym HCKEGS as a reminder of the basic innate drives necessary for a domestic cat's daily happiness and fulfilment: Hunt, Catch, Kill, Eat, Groom, Sleep. A significant portion of a cat's driving force is linked to the first term in particular, as they are natural-born hunters whose instincts persist even when they spend most of their time lounging with their owners.

'As anyone who has ever been around a cat for any length of time well knows, cats have enormous patience with the limitations of humankind.'

Cleveland Amory

Living with humans requires cats to make significant compromises such as limiting their freedom of movement and sharing their territory, among other things. Therefore, it is important to provide your cat with daily structured play and when he meows or makes other sounds to get your attention, that you respond to his invitations.

As Jackson Galaxy emphasizes, 'Play isn't a luxury, something that is a fun diversion if and when you have time ... If you have a cat, you have interactive toys and you use them for daily play sessions ... they are a physical and behavioural necessity.' Regardless of whether your cat brings live prey into the house, it's your responsibility to engage in structured play-hunting sessions with your cat daily, not just when you're feeling bored or guilty about neglecting your pet.

THAT'S MINE, GET OFF

GUARDING RESOURCES AND PROTECTING TERRITORY ARE INNATE DRIVES THAT CAN OFTEN DOMINATE THE BEHAVIOUR AND WELLBEING OF A DOMESTICATED CAT, ESPECIALLY IN MULTI-CAT HOUSEHOLDS.

Feline expert, author and star of the hit TV show, *My Cat from Hell*, Jackson Galaxy has even gone as far as to claim that 'Many, if not most, of the problems' that his cat clients experience '(with the exception of undiagnosed physical issues), could be boiled down to territorial anxiety'.

It doesn't matter if the threat is real or perceived. Resource and territory guarding is commonly observed in domestic cats where they exhibit aggressive or defensive behaviour towards humans or other animals who approach or try to take away something they consider valuable. This valuable resource can be food, toys, bedding, a person, or any other items the cat considers important.

If your cat feels that his resources or territory are under threat, he may display aggressive behaviour like hissing, growling, swatting or biting to protect his stuff. Some cats may also use body language like flattening their ears, arching their back, or puffing up their fur to intimidate potential threats.

Conflict over resources can commonly occur in multi-pet households. You may think you and your furry enclave are living in perfect harmony, but the reality can feel different to the members of your imagined feline idyll. Domestic cats can adapt well to large free-living groups such as a feral colony, because they have the freedom to choose their social interactions within a relatively larger living area. But when two or more cats are smushed together in a small urban home, then not only will they face the stress of competition for territory outside the house, but they may also feel that they are competing for resources within it.

> 'Co-habiting cats may appear to be compatible but often this is not the case. Conflict can occur very subtly with one cat blocking access to food, litter boxes, or a cat flap, or perhaps ousting another cat from preferred resting spots around the home.'
>
> Dr Sarah Brown, *The Cat: A Natural History*

Resource guarding in cats can become a serious problem if it's ignored. Unless it is addressed early on, it can escalate and become a safety issue. Since prevention is better than cure, make sure your cat has access to sufficient, individual resources like food, water, litter boxes and toys, and that these items are in suitable quiet places with minimal human traffic.

The scent glands of cats emit a distinct and individual pheromone that serves various purposes such as demarcating territory and conveying social hierarchy and sexual availability. To maintain their marking, cats repeatedly return to their preferred locations, such as entrances, nesting spots, high-traffic areas and territorial boundaries. Awareness of these boundaries and clearly defined territories often resolves disputes without the need for cats to engage in physical confrontation.

If your cat is already displaying resource-guarding
behaviour or spraying inappropriately, you should speak
to a veterinarian or a professional animal behaviourist.
They can help identify the underlying causes and develop
a plan to modify your cat's behaviour through positive
reinforcement training.

Never use punishment or physical force to address resource
guarding in cats, as this can worsen the behaviour and
damage the relationship between the cat and its owner.
Instead, use positive reinforcement techniques like
rewarding the cat with treats or praise for good behaviour.

> 'Resource guarding arises from underlying anxiety, so,
> when your cat displays aggressive behaviour — hissing,
> swatting and attacking — and the person or animal
> backs away, the resource guarding behaviour becomes
> negatively reinforced. Without proper intervention, it
> can become your cat's go-to behavioural response.'
>
> Dr Pam Perry

YES,

I'M TALKING TO YOU

DID YOU KNOW THAT ADULT CATS TYPICALLY DON'T USE VOCALIZATIONS (OTHER THAN HISSING AND CATERWAULING) TO COMMUNICATE WITH OTHER CATS? THEY HAVE DEVELOPED THEIR TRADEMARK 'MEOW' SPECIFICALLY FOR COMMUNICATING WITH HUMANS. THIS IMPLIES THAT OVER THE COURSE OF THOUSANDS OF YEARS OF COHABITATION WITH HUMANS, CATS HAVE LEARNED HOW TO MANIPULATE, ENTERTAIN AND CAPTIVATE US WITH THEIR REPERTOIRE OF MEOWS.

At the same time, humans have also learned how to train cats to recognize certain human vocalizations, as well as to understand our emotional state through our tone of voice. It's truly remarkable how two distinct species have learned to communicate with each other in such a nuanced way. This means that when you talk to your cat and she responds with a meow, a genuine form of communication is occurring between you and your pet. Your cat is a highly intelligent and autonomous creature who has developed a unique language for interacting with humans, so you should interact with her in a way that respects and acknowledges this.

It's true that cats have a wide range of meows that they use for various purposes, and as their owner, you're likely to be the best at interpreting what each one means. These meows aren't a figment of your imagination or a result of anthropomorphizing your cat. Cats have learned to use vocalizations to get what they want from humans. They've discovered that humans can be trained to respond to certain meows, just as we've learned to recognize their various forms of body language.

There's a meow for almost every situation, whether it's a request to be let in or out, for you to open a tin of tuna or as an expression of affection. In addition to meows, cats have also developed a 'silent meow' that they use to appeal to their more dominant human family members. While it's not really silent (just too high-pitched for human ears), this type of meow is known for being particularly persuasive and is often accompanied by a tap of the paw.

> "'Meow'" means "Woof" in cat.'"
>
> George Carlin

Don't assume that every meow is a demand for food. Sometimes, a simple short meow can just be a casual 'Hello'. While genetics, personality and life experiences can all influence a cat's meowing repertoire, ultimately, these sounds are effective because they get results from humans. If we didn't respond to their meows, cats wouldn't continue to use them as a means of communication. So, pay attention and try to understand what she is saying.

In 1944, New York psychologist Mildred Moelk discovered that cats meow differently to people than to fellow cats. She categorized 16 sounds used in cat-human and cat-cat communication, which are still applicable today for understanding feline vocalizations. They first appeared in her paper 'Vocalizing in the House Cat: A Phonetic and Functional Study' in the April 1944 *Journal of Comparative Psychology*.

Moelk's research showed that cats use a range of vocal variations such as duration, intensity, tone, pitch, roughness, stress and speed to convey their messages. As cat owners know from first-hand experience, a cat's meows can range from gentle and persuasive to insistent and demanding. However, some animal behaviourists have suggested that these variations may not be as nuanced as previously thought. The prevailing theory now is that cats have learned that if they meow with enough intensity, pitch, and repetition, they can easily grab human attention and get what they want.

Moelk organized the vocalizations she observed into three patterns based on how cats formed the sounds:

1. **MURMUR PATTERNS:** consonant made with mouth closed, breath passes through the nose.

2. **VOWEL PATTERNS:** breath passes through the open mouth as it closes.

3. **STRAINED INTENSITY PATTERNS:** voiced breath forced through the mouth which is held wide open.

An apostrophe (') means an emphasis, most often from inhalation, and a long dash (—) is a sustained sound.

MURMUR PATTERNS
Express greeting or satisfaction,
e.g., 'Hello' or 'Pay attention to me'.

1. Purr ('hrn-rhn-'hrn-rhn)
2. Request or Greeting ('mhrn'hr'hrn)
3. Call ('mhrn)
4. Acknowledgment or Confirmation ('mhng)

VOWEL PATTERNS

Requests or complaints, e.g., 'Give me' or 'Please give me'.

1. Demand ('mhrn-a'—ou)

2. Begging Demand ('mhrn-a—ou—)

3. Bewilderment ('maou?)

4. Complaint ('mhng-a—ou)

5. Mating Cry – mild form ('mhrn-a—ou)

6. Anger Wail (wa—ou—)

STRAINED INTENSITY PATTERNS

Arousal or stress, e.g., 'I like' or 'I don't like'.

1. Growl (grrrrr)

2. Snarl (aye–a)

3. Mating Cry (ooy-ooy-a)

4. Pain Scream (aye-ee)

5. Refusal Rasp (aye–aye–aye)

6. Spitting (fff-tu)

Meows aside, if you want to understand the bigger picture, you need to read the more complex and nuanced forms of communication that cats use to communicate with each other as well as with humans: subtle facial expressions, tail positions, ear positions and other body language indicators. Additionally, cats have an intricate language of smells – a rich source of information that is, sadly, beyond our human olfactory capabilities.

IS THAT ME?
NAH

IN 1970, PSYCHOLOGIST GORDON GALLUP CONDUCTED A WIDELY KNOWN STUDY CALLED THE 'MIRROR SELF-REFLECTION TEST' WHICH WAS PUBLISHED IN THE JOURNAL, *THE COGNITIVE ANIMAL*. DURING THE STUDY, RESEARCHERS PLACED AN UNSCENTED NON-IRRITANT RED SPOT ON THE FACE OF A SEDATED ANIMAL AND HYPOTHESIZED THAT IF, UPON WAKING, THE ANIMAL TOUCHED THE SPOT, IT WOULD INDICATE RECOGNITION OF ITS ALTERED APPEARANCE AND THUS, SELF-RECOGNITION.

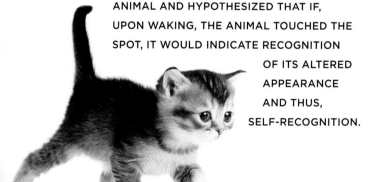

This self-recognition skill comes naturally to humans: between the ages of 18 to 24 months, a typically developing baby gains this ability without being taught. While some animals, such as chimpanzees, orangutans, gorillas, bonobo apes, bottlenose dolphins, killer whales, Asian elephants and magpies have been shown to pass the mirror test, domestic cats have not been extensively tested for this ability. The few tests that have been conducted found no evidence of self-recognition in cats.

One study published in the journal *Behavioural Processes* in 2015 found that most of the cats in the study did not show signs of recognizing themselves in the mirror. However, some of the cats did exhibit behaviours such as touching the mirror with their paws, but that wasn't interpreted as an indication of self-recognition.

Cats certainly recognise another cat in the mirror, but they don't realise it's them, despite all the cute viral cat videos that suggest otherwise. When encountering their reflection, some cats may hide behind the mirror to look for another cat, while others may completely ignore it. Some may exhibit aggressive or wary behaviour towards what seems like another cat that can perfectly mimic their own gestures. While this may appear like the cat is playfully interacting with itself, its body language is that of defence mode: the puffed-out tail and low ear position are a response to the perceived 'threat' of the reflection.

> 'It takes a good deal of sophisticated integration of information about yourself and your own movements and what you're seeing in front of you in that glass.'
>
> Diana Reiss, animal psychologist

Overall, the question of whether cats have self-awareness remains a topic of ongoing scientific inquiry. Further research is needed to fully understand the nature and extent of their cognitive abilities, especially since cats are motivated more by smell than sight. Also, in the fifty years since the mirror test was devised, many scientists have argued that self-awareness exists on a spectrum rather than being binary, and that we judge animals and humans using the same metrics at our peril.

Many ethologists today would no doubt argue that our priority should be to move beyond grading animals intellectually and to focus instead on creating a world in which we finally recognise that the rights of every living creature are as sacred as our own.

WHAT'S THAT
SMELL?

RECENT RESEARCH HAS REVEALED THAT THE HUMAN NOSE HARBOURS APPROXIMATELY 6 MILLION SCENT RECEPTORS IN ROUGHLY 400 VARIETIES, ENABLING US TO DETECT AT LEAST ONE TRILLION DISTINCT ODOURS. THIS IS A SIGNIFICANT ADVANCEMENT COMPARED TO SCIENTISTS' PREVIOUS ESTIMATE OF ABOUT 10,000 SMELLS.

However, cats possess around 200 million scent receptors, over thirty times more than humans, making it impossible for us to comprehend the richness of their olfactory world.

Given that cats are born deaf and blind, their sense of smell plays a critical role in their survival, especially during the early days when they use it to locate their mother's nipple. The mother also rubs her scent onto her kittens to identify them. Smell is the predominant component of feline communication, which is why rubbing to exchange scents is such a common practice.

Compared to humans, cats have a relatively low number of taste receptors on their tongues. As a result, their sense of hunger is primarily stimulated by the smell, rather than the flavour of their food. This explains why cats with respiratory infections or nasal blockages may lose their appetite – without a sense of smell, they don't experience the hunger-inducing effects of aroma.

Scent markers reveal which cats have marked or sprayed urine and how long ago, as well as their gender and social status. It enables them to distinguish potential threats from benign ones and provides precise information about the opposite sex, aiding them in locating prey and determining food edibility. Your cat's sense of smell is so sensitive that she can detect odours that are not even perceptible to humans. For example, she can detect the scent of a mouse from several feet away, whereas we would have to rely on our eyesight. Scientists estimate cats can smell their food from between 38 to 47 metres away (roughly the length of three-four buses).

> 'Scents are a driving force in cats' lives and make up a large part of how they understand and navigate the world.'
>
> Deborah Brannon

The Flehmen Reaction is a clever technique that cats use to gather a wealth of information about other felines in the neighbourhood. The term 'flehmen' originates from the German word 'flehmen,' which means to bare the upper teeth, and also from the Upper Saxon German word 'flemmen,' meaning to look spiteful.

When a cat is 'doing a Flehmen,' she stops, raises her head, and opens her mouth, visibly curling back her upper lip to expose her front teeth. She transfers the smell chemicals into the Jacobson's organ, which is an olfactory sense organ found in many animals. This organ is located behind the front teeth, and by pressing her tongue against the roof of her mouth, allows her to 'taste' the smell. Without affecting her regular breathing, she can maintain this expression for several seconds to determine the age, sex and reproductive status of the felines in the vicinity.

Interestingly, male cats, also known as toms, tend to use this behaviour more frequently than females, but it is still a common behaviour for both sexes.

This response is not limited to domestic cats, as it is also commonly observed in various species of wild cats, such as lions and tigers and in a wide range of animals, including horses, zebras, giraffes, goats, elks, snakes, giant pandas and even hedgehogs.

> Cats are not just using their sense of smell to identify who you are, they're also using it to determine how they feel about you.'
>
> Pam Johnson-Bennett, *Think Like a Cat*

Being sensitive to the importance of smell in your cat's life will help you communicate better with her. For example, you might consider avoiding wearing perfume or aftershave, which is overpowering and masks your natural scent, which is what your cat really wants to smell. When you bring new carpets, curtains or furniture into your home they will emit dozens of strange smells and chemicals, so don't be surprised if your cat is attracted to them and rubs herself against them frequently. When you tickle your cat under her chin, cheeks and the base of her tail, the primary appeal for her is that you are exchanging and mingling scents.

I LOVE
YOU

ALTHOUGH EACH CAT HAS ITS OWN UNIQUE
WAY OF SHOWING AFFECTION, THERE ARE SOME
COMMON SIGNS YOU CAN LOOK OUT FOR. THESE
INCLUDE PURRING, GROOMING,
KNEADING, NOSE-TOUCHING,
HEAD-BUTTING (KNOWN AS
BUNTING), BRINGING GIFTS,
SLOW BLINKING, FOLLOWING
YOU AROUND AND
EXPOSING THE BELLY.

However, some gestures of love may be unique and personal to your cat, so pay close attention to how she interacts with you. Remember that cats do not gesture accidentally and all body language and physical contact hold meaning. So, stay attentive and keep an eye out for the many ways your cat shows her love.

PURRING: this is one of the most recognizable signs of a cat's contentment. When you pet or hold her and she begins to purr, it's a clear indication that she feels relaxed in your presence. There has been much debate about how cats produce their purr, which continues without interruption while the cat breathes in and out.

'Experts had various theories, but the most current information is that the purr is created by contractions of the laryngeal muscles and diaphragm, which create pressure in the glottis.'

Pam Johnson-Bennett, *Think Like a Cat*

Cats also purr to self-soothe when they are in pain. Studies have shown that the vibrational frequency of the purr – 25 hertz – promotes wound healing and increased bone density and muscle mass.

GROOMING: familiar cats groom each other to reinforce their social bonds, strengthen their hierarchy and alleviate stress. If your cat licks your face or nibbles your fingers, for example, this grooming behaviour demonstrates a deep level of trust and affection.

KNEADING: nursing kittens instinctively knead their mother's soft abdomen to encourage the production of milk. Kneading remains a sign of contentment into adulthood because of this strong association between soft surfaces (such as cushions or your body) with receiving food and comfort. So, cats commonly show affection by kneading their owners, combining self-soothing with territorial marking. Basically, they never miss an opportunity to label their stuff!

Kneading transfers your cat's scent onto you through scent glands on her paws. Female cats also knead before going into heat to signal to male cats that they are ready to mate. Kneading might also be a residual ritual, similar to a dog's circling behaviour before lying down, to flatten grass and get rid of small critters.

NOSE TOUCHING: although kittens are born blind and deaf, the sense of smell and the touch receptors on the nose are in full working order. They make early contact with their mother and their litter mates through nose touching. Once learned, nose touching is never forgotten and continues to be used throughout the cat's life.

BUNTING: cats often express affection by head-butting or rubbing their heads against you, known as bunting. Through this behaviour, your cat marks you with her scent and

demonstrates her trust in you. All cats, wild and domestic, engage in bunting to strengthen social bonds and scent mark other animals as safe.

BRINGING GIFTS: while it may not be the most pleasant sign of affection, cats often bring their owners 'gifts' in the form of dead animals or toys. Don't punish her for bringing you animals, dead or alive. She's only following her instincts and it's a sign that she trusts you and wants to share her resources with you.

BLINKING SLOWLY AT YOU: if your feline companion squints and gradually closes her eyes for a few seconds, it's a sign that she is giving you a 'kitty kiss' because she is feeling calm and secure around you. Even feral cats do this to indicate that they are not a danger to other cats. Cats use their eyes to convey a great deal of information: humans staring at them with wide eyes can be perceived as a threat. However, the gradual blink signifies that they have confidence in you not to harm them while their eyes are closed. You can also give your cat a slow blink and see if she reciprocates.

FOLLOWING YOU AROUND: If your cat follows you around the house or sits near you when you're working or relaxing, it's a sign that she enjoys your company and wants to be close to you. If she lies across your laptop keyboard to stop you working, not only is she attention-seeking but also benefitting from the warmth!

ROLLING ON HER BACK: cats only roll on their back to expose their vulnerable bellies when they are feeling relaxed and trusting. However, this isn't necessarily an invitation for you to start rubbing her tummy. The fact that she does it in your company is a plus, but she may simply be enjoying a solo back rub. Female cats also roll when they are in heat. According to animal behaviourist, Hilary Feldman: 'Females roll primarily in the presence of adult males, demonstrating a readiness to mate'. Feldman's experimental observations have also confirmed that 'males roll near adult males as a form of subordinate behaviour' and 'that rolling may act as passive submission and inhibits the development of overt aggression'. So, cats may roll both to placate us and to exhibit passive submission.

I'M RELAXED AND HAPPY

WHEN A CAT IS RELAXED AND HAPPY, SHE WILL
TYPICALLY HAVE HER EARS FACING FORWARD
OR SLIGHTLY TO THE SIDE (NOT PINNED BACK OR
FLATTENED) AND HER WHISKERS NATURALLY FANNING
OUT AND POINTING DOWNWARDS. HER FRONT FEET
WILL BE FOLDED TOWARDS HER BODY OR HER BODY
WILL BE ELONGATED AND LEGS STRETCHED OUT. HER
TAIL WILL BE CURLED UP NEXT TO HER BODY, AND
HER EYES WILL APPEAR SLEEPY, WITH OVAL PUPILS.
YOU MAY HEAR HER PURRING AND SEE HER CURLING
INTO A BALL OR STRETCHING OUT ON HER BACK,
INDICATING A HIGH LEVEL OF COMFORT AND TRUST.

41

While it may be tempting to rub her belly when she exposes it, this is not always an invitation for affection. Cats may tolerate a few strokes before becoming uncomfortable and ready to scratch with their back legs. It's essential to respect a cat's need for relaxation and not interrupt her blissful state with unnecessary attention.

So, instead of always satisfying your urge to cuddle, smooth and stroke, take a moment to appreciate your cat's contentedness and spare a thought for her needs. She may look adorable and inviting, but it's crucial to respect her space and boundaries.

> 'By accepting our petting, cats are doing more than enjoying themselves: in their minds, they are almost certainly engaging in a social ritual that is reinforcing the bond with their owner.'
>
> John Bradshaw, *Cat Sense*

A relaxed and contented cat will display her happiness through her whiskers, which naturally fan out and point downwards. Conversely, an alert, excited, or angry cat will often push her whiskers out to the side and forward, in a 'jazz hands' motion. When a cat is feeling threatened, she may draw her whiskers along the sides of her face as a defensive mechanism.

Despite being famously fastidious, cats need very little in material terms, but these things must cater to their instinctive behaviours. Cats thrive on routine and require their own designated areas to feel protected, nutritious food and water, a comfortable temperature, a suitable scratching post, regular playtime (at least twice daily), toys for amusement and a hygienic litter box. Also, they love affection and snuggles when they're in the mood.

However, although your cat needs all these factors to be present before she can feel safe and comfortable, she also needs the freedom to indulge her natural instincts and to feel in control of her environment.

Every responsible cat owner provides a scratching post, but have you also considered creating a vertical space for her, such as cat trees, shelves, or window perches? Cats love to climb and perch up high, so creating vertical space in your home can give your cat the opportunity

43

to indulge this instinct. If you've ever wondered why cats get stuck in trees, it's because their powerful hind legs and curved claws are ideal for climbing up (to gain a vantage point and to escape predators) but not so well suited for manoeuvring down again.

Another important consideration is that cats are natural predators, so they need hiding spots – cardboard boxes, paper bags or covered beds – to feel safe and secure. Cats have a natural inclination to avoid conflict and seek refuge in hiding rather than engaging in direct confrontation. When faced with environmental or psychological threats, cats tend to reduce their activity levels. Additionally, having access to a small hiding spot allows a cat to remain unnoticed by potential prey, minimizing the amount of body odour that could give away their presence to mice or birds.

If any of these requirements are missing, your cat will feel out of sorts and instead of settling near you, she may pace restlessly. If she is actively frustrated, she will fixate on the source of her annoyance, which should give you a big clue. Conversely, if your cat is feeling playful, it's a healthy sign that she is happy and content.

When you play (see pages 74-75), you need to include interactive toys that can satisfy her need to hunt, chase, and pounce. Toys such as feather wands, laser pointers, and puzzle feeders can help keep her mentally and physically stimulated.

I'M FEELING ANXIOUS AND
STRESSED

AS WE'VE ALREADY LEARNED, JACKSON GALAXY
USES THE ACRONYM HCKEGS (HUNT, CATCH, KILL,
EAT, GROOM, SLEEP) IN HIS BOOK, *TOTAL CAT MOJO*,
TO REMIND CAT OWNERS OF THE BASIC INNATE
DRIVES WHICH MUST BE SATISFIED DAILY FOR A
DOMESTIC CAT TO LEAD A HAPPY AND FULFILLED
LIFE. BARRING ILLNESS, ANY DISTURBANCE TO THESE
KEY INGREDIENTS TO FELINE HAPPINESS WILL BE MET
WITH BEHAVIOUR THAT EXPRESSES ANXIETY.

Hiding is often one of the first things cat owners notice when their cat is feeling anxious. Cats may hide in small, enclosed spaces like under the bed, in a closet, or behind furniture. Dr Karen Becker, a holistic veterinarian, explains why cats tend to hide when they are stressed: 'Cats are hardwired to hide when they're feeling threatened or insecure. This is because in the wild, cats are both predators and prey, and they need to be able to hide from potential predators while they are hunting or resting. When a cat is feeling anxious or stressed, their natural instinct is to find a safe place to hide until they feel more secure'.

'Cats are creatures of habit, and any disruption to their routine or environment can lead to anxiety and stress.'

Pam Johnson-Bennett

Cats use hiding as a natural coping mechanism, and it's crucial to acknowledge their need for privacy and security.

Nevertheless, if you observe that your cat is hiding more frequently or avoiding contact with you, it could indicate that she is experiencing anxiety or stress. This is particularly valid if your cat is typically extroverted and sociable.

Excessive grooming is another common behaviour that cats may exhibit when they are stressed. Cats are known for being fastidious groomers and they often use it as a means of self-soothing and reducing stress levels. However, if you notice that your cat's grooming habits are excessive and leading to hair loss or bald patches, it could indicate an underlying medical condition or anxiety.

Changes in appetite are another indication that your cat may be experiencing stress or anxiety. Cats who are feeling stressed may become picky eaters or lose interest in their food, while others may begin to overeat.

When cats feel threatened or anxious, they may display aggression through excessive vocalisations and behaviours such as hissing, growling, biting, or scratching. Changes in the environment, such as the introduction of a new pet or a move to a new home, can be a significant source of stress for cats and may manifest as aggression towards people or other animals. But generally, cats express their anxiety quietly, withdrawing themselves, playing a less active role in the household and suffering in silence, which is much harder to spot than active aggression.

'Anxiety is the most common emotional problem in cats, and it's important for cat owners to be aware of the signs and take steps to help their cats feel more secure and calm.'

Dr Marty Becker

If the litter box is in the wrong place, dirty, or using litter that your cat doesn't like, she won't use it and that alone will be sufficient to cause her stress. But stress can also lead to litter box issues (such as going to the toilet outside the box or using it more often) even when the conditions seem perfect. When a cat visits her litter tray frequently but fails to produce any urine, it indicates a severe emergency. Her bladder might be blocked and require urgent medical attention.

Anxiety is also expressed by changes in sleeping habits, either sleeping excessively as a coping mechanism or struggling to get enough rest because of hyperstimulation. An overstimulated cat who refuses to stay asleep can keep the entire household awake as she patters around in the middle of the night. This ratchets up the stress level for everyone, which will inevitably feed back to your cat and make her even more anxious. Don't tolerate disrupted sleep – seek advice from your vet.

I'M VERY
AFRAID

WHEN A CAT IS VERY AFRAID, HIS BODY LANGUAGE CAN COMMUNICATE HIS FEAR QUITE CLEARLY. HE WILL LOWER HIS HEAD AND BODY, TWITCH HIS EARS TO LISTEN FOR POTENTIAL THREATS (OR PRESS THEM FLAT AGAINST HIS HEAD), AND RETRACT HIS WHISKERS ALONGSIDE HIS FACE. THE TAIL IS CARRIED LOW, TOUCHING THE GROUND, AND THE CAT WILL MAINTAIN THIS POSITION WHILE QUIETLY ASSESSING THE SITUATION.

A defensive cat will often hold his head to the side and make darting sidelong glances rather than look directly at the aggressor. By making himself appear smaller, the cat tries to appear less threatening. However, if he feels cornered or needs to be more assertive, he will switch to defensive anger and will stand up straight, arch his back and fluff out his tail to make himself appear larger. As the cat's anxiety increases, his eyes will remain open and unblinking, with pupils dilated into an oval or circle.

'The problem with cats is that they get the exact same look on their face whether they see a moth or an axe-murderer.'

Paula Poundstone

He may start to cower and look miserable while his tail remains still or moves slowly from side to side at the tip. If a cat is afraid, he may crouch down low to the ground or try to find a hiding place where they feel safe. In some cases, a cat may tremble or shake when he is very afraid.

If you notice your cat displaying these behaviours, offer him verbal and physical reassurance and try to identify the source of his anxiety. Perhaps there is a stranger outside (or inside) the house, or there has been a change in his immediate environment. Like humans, cats can become stressed for various reasons, but change is usually the most common cause.

> 'A terrified cat is not a nasty cat. She's a frightened cat, and she doesn't know how else to react except to be scared and reactive.'
>
> Vicky Halls, cat behaviourist

To divert your cat's attention from the perceived threat and help reduce his adrenaline levels, try a play session. Additionally, you could create a peaceful environment by playing calming music or reducing noise levels in the house, such as turning down the TV volume or asking everyone to quieten down. In case the anxiety persists, you could consider using a pheromone diffuser. This straightforward device releases calming hormones into the air, which can signal to your cat that everything is safe.

Don't punish your cat for 'misbehaving' during a stressful episode (e.g., showing aggression, peeing on your bed). In *Total Cat Mojo*, Jackson Galaxy makes a distinction between time-out and kitty jail. If you lock your cat out of your bedroom for peeing on the bed, it won't teach him not to do it again because he won't make the association. But it will increase his levels of stress. Instead, he recommends a time-out: 'You can lead him to a small, confined environment, with lights down low, no sounds, no stimulation, no nothing. This decompression zone allowed that cat to re-enter his own body's orbit ... get your cat out of DEFCON 1 ... out of fight or flight, and back into the real world.'

I'M WARNING
YOU

CATS CAN DISPLAY A VARIETY OF BEHAVIOURS
WHEN THEY ARE ANGRY OR AFRAID, AND THERE IS
MUCH OVERLAP IN THE WAY THEIR BODY LANGUAGE
CONVEYS THESE TWO EMOTIONS. WITH BOTH, THE
EARS ARE FLATTENED AGAINST THE HEAD AND THE
EYES ARE WIDE WITH DILATED PUPILS. THE CAT MAY
ALSO HISS OR GROWL WHEN FEELING ANGRY OR
THREATENED AND TWITCH OR SWISH THEIR TAIL
FROM SIDE TO SIDE.

When expressing angry aggression, the cat stands with his body arched and his fur standing on end. When expressing fear aggression, the body is crouched low to the ground, usually facing sideways, but the head and front paws point towards the perceived threat. In this conflicted body position, your cat is ready to flee and to fight.

When a cat reaches this level of vulnerability, feels cornered or trapped, and senses that an attack is imminent, that's when you'll witness warning signs. The cat will use these to indicate that he doesn't want to fight (since avoiding violence is safer and more desirable than the risk of sustaining life-threatening injuries).

Remember that every cat is different, and some cats may display different behaviours when they are angry. If you are unsure about your cat's behaviour, it's best to give him space and avoid touching him until he has calmed down. Even if you approach him with soothing words and try to pet him, you are likely to make things worse.

> 'A cat who acts aggressively isn't being mean or defiant or taking pleasure in watching you recoil in fear. A cat acts aggressively because he feels he has no other choice … It isn't fair to merely categorize a cat as being "aggressive" … because any animal is potentially capable of aggression under the right circumstances.'
>
> Pam Johnson-Bennett, *Think Like a Cat*

53

Aggression is a crucial part of your cat's defences, without which he would be unable to survive in the wild. It enables him to catch hunt food, defend territory, find a mate, protect himself from attack and, in the case of a female cat, defend her kittens.

The warning signs leading up to aggression are unmistakable (although they may be cut short or missed out altogether if the cat's fear and threat levels escalate too quickly). The most obvious is a low growling sound. The body language signs include skin twitching, tail lashing and paw smacks without claws (sheathed claws). At this stage, if you or the target of his aggression don't retreat, he will have no choice but to attack with full weaponry – claws and teeth.

You are most likely to witness fear aggression when you take your cat to the vet. Not only can cats become aggressive when they are sick, but the unfamiliar smells, sounds and other animals in the veterinary clinic can easily put them on high alert.

> 'Pay attention to the cat's posture and warning signals. Don't attempt to handle a cat displaying aggression.'
>
> Pam Johnson-Bennett, *Think Like a Cat*

I'M
CONFUSED/
CONFLICTED

WHEN A CAT IS CONFUSED AND CONFLICTED, IT MAY DISPLAY VARIOUS BODY LANGUAGE CUES. FOR EXAMPLE, THE CAT MAY TILT ITS HEAD TO THE SIDE, AS IF TRYING TO FIGURE SOMETHING OUT.

Its eyes may be wide open, and its pupils may be dilated, indicating that it is trying to take in as much information as possible. The cat's ears may be held partially back or to the side, indicating uncertainty or anxiety. The tail may twitch or flick rapidly, which can be a sign of nervousness or agitation.

In some cases, the cat may freeze in place or move slowly and cautiously, as if unsure of what to do next. He may also groom himself excessively or engage in displacement behaviours, such as licking or scratching, which can be a sign of stress or anxiety. Overall, when a cat is confused and conflicted, his body language may be more subdued and cautious than when he is feeling confident and relaxed.

> 'Cats that are experiencing stress often become more vocal. A new pet or baby, a move or changes to the home, an illness or the loss of a loved one can turn your cat into a talker.'
>
> Sandy Eckstein

Excessive vocalisation can be a sign of confusion, especially in older cats. As cats age, they may begin to wail due to disorientation and sensory loss (including hearing, smell, and sight) or dementia. Night-time yowling is common in older cats, as they may feel confused, lonely, or bored and crave attention from their owners. This excessive vocalization may also be due to medical issues such as high blood pressure, hyperthyroidism (causing constant hunger), chronic pain, or a slow-growing brain tumour called a meningioma.

If you adopt an older cat who is accustomed to living with other feline companions, he may wail while searching for his housemates who are no longer present. Alternatively, he may wake up feeling disoriented and uncertain of his surroundings.

Cats can develop dementia. It is known as Cognitive Dysfunction Syndrome (CDS) which in cats generally manifests slowly over time and may be misdiagnosed as other health issues. While it is common for older cats to sleep for extended periods, if your cat is sleeping during times when he is typically awake, or awake during times when he usually sleeps, this may be indicative of CDS. If he seems disoriented, stares off into space for extended periods of time, aimlessly wanders in familiar surroundings, seems confused while searching for his food or litter box or appears to have forgotten previous learned behaviours or daily routines, such as grooming, seek advice from your vet.

'I've seen cats become confused and disoriented as they age, and it's important to provide them with a comfortable and familiar environment to help them cope with the changes.'

Pam Johnson-Bennett, *Think Like a Cat*

I'M SO FOCUSED RIGHT NOW

DOMESTIC CATS POSSESS AN INNATE HUNTING INSTINCT, MAKING THEM NATURAL PREDATORS WHO EXHIBIT INTENSE CONCENTRATION WHILE IN PURSUIT OF PREY.

During the hunt, your cat's eyes widen, his pupils narrow, his ears and whiskers prick forward and his body is angled towards his target. He may crouch low to the ground, coiling his hind legs beneath his body as he stalks his prey.

If he isn't actively stalking but is highly stimulated, he will commonly sit upright with his ears pointing upward and being attentive. He may have detected the sound or scent of a mouse or he might be anticipating that any moment you will open a pouch of cat food and call him for supper. This is a good posture for a cat. It shows he's engaged with his surroundings in a positive (not fearful) way, is happy and energetic.

Your cat's physiology is perfectly suited for hunting. Despite their adorable appearance, your cat's big, round eyes serve a crucial purpose. They belong to a highly specialized nocturnal predator who requires maximum light collection. The retina inside his eyes is six times more sensitive than ours in low light, allowing him to see in near darkness at the expense of sharpness and colour perception. On the other hand, cheetahs, which hunt during the day, have smaller eyes relative to their head size.

A single mouse can supply a cat with roughly thirty calories of energy. To survive in the wild, an average-sized domestic cat would need to consume around eight mice daily. This would take up to thirty hunting attempts each day to meet his daily meat requirement, although, it would account for less than twenty percent of his waking hours. Due to their primarily carnivorous diet, cats have a shorter digestive tract than herbivores or omnivores. Unlike animals that require a lengthy digestive tract for breaking down plants, a shorter digestive tract is sufficient for digesting meat. This design allows cats to maintain a lower weight, which enables them to run, jump and hunt more easily.

However, since all your cat's food needs are met by you, how does he spend all that spare time? Most of his daytime hours are devoted to grooming, gazing out the window and napping. While outdoor cats will likely engage in hunting activities, indoor cats require at least three play-hunting sessions each day to simulate moving prey. It doesn't have to be fancy – you can use a ball, mouse or feather attached to a string or wand. Each session only needs to last about ten minutes, but it's important to allow your cat to successfully catch his 'prey' during these sessions for a fulfilling experience.

> 'We talked of mice, the cat and I, and of the importance of napping.'
>
> Catherine Gilbert Murdock

Have you ever wondered why your well-fed cat enjoys hunting and frequently presents you with small rodents and birds, yet never seems to eat them? It turns out that kittens

have an innate hunting and chasing instinct that they refine through play. They practice their skills by stalking, ambushing and pursuing their littermates. However, they only learn that their prey is food if their mother teaches them. If the mother never brings home prey to feed her kittens (which breeders typically avoid before vaccination), they don't learn the connection between hunting and eating. After weaning, they are usually sent to new homes and spend their lives hunting for pleasure rather than for survival.

'A lot of what their eyes are picking up on is movement. And they have lots of specialist nerves that pick up on movement: downward, sideways, diagonally, things getting larger, things getting smaller and especially in the peripheral vision, around the sides.

John Bradshaw

If your cat is watching a bird through the window that he can't reach, his teeth may start chattering involuntarily as an expression of excitement or frustration. Domestic and wild cats alike deliver a 'kill bite' to the back of their prey's neck, puncturing the spinal cord where it connects to the skull. Cats may use a chattering motion to locate this vulnerable area, so when your cat is chattering his teeth while watching birds from behind the curtains, it's likely a reflex action in his attempt to deliver this fatal bite.

Before pouncing on their prey, cats have been observed making noises like those of their intended victim. This behaviour is believed to either distract the prey or mask any rustling sounds made by the cat as he winds himself up to spring.

Compared to humans, cats have a limited sense of taste and fewer taste buds. Their olfactory system is primarily focused on hunting and detecting prey rather than enjoying the nuanced flavours of a rodent snack. For cats, the scent of food is more critical than its taste. Nonetheless, cats have a taste receptor that humans lack, specifically for adenosine triphosphate (ATP), a compound that provides energy to drive various processes in living cells. This receptor acts as a signal for meat, which is the only food that cats eat in the wild.

> 'After dark, all cats are leopards.'
>
> Alison Davies

I'M A GOOD
BOY

LIKE DOGS AND CHILDREN, THE BEST WAY TO
TRAIN CATS IS BY POSITIVE REINFORCEMENT
– REWARDING DESIRED BEHAVIOUR WHILE
IGNORING NEGATIVE BEHAVIOUR.

WHAT IS MY CAT REALLY THINKING?

Although it may seem like common sense, many cat owners inadvertently reinforce problematic behaviours by creating the conditions that cause them and then resorting to punishment. Unfortunately, punishment only serves to frighten and confuse cats.

Fear is never an acceptable form of correction for cats, and even if it were, reprimands and punishments are only effective when they immediately follow the undesirable behaviour. Punishment even a few seconds later will traumatize your cat, but he won't connect it with whatever it was he was doing. As a result, you'll end up with a terrified and confused cat who still engages in the behaviour you're trying to prevent. Dr Tony Buffington, DVM, PhD, Clinical Professor UC Davis School of Veterinary Medicine, advises: 'If you do catch your cat making a mistake, it is better for both of you to create a distraction by making a loud noise or throwing something (NOT at the cat!) that will attract its attention, but not toward you.'

If you're looking to train your cat in a particular domestic skill, like swallowing a worming pill, or deterring him from certain behaviours, you must recognize that cats react best to positive reinforcement and praise. They do not respond well to any kind of force, including physical punishment, being squirted with water, or receiving loud verbal scolding. Dr Tony Buffington's assertion that, 'We tend to see shouting and punishment as forms of "conflict resolution"; cats see these as life-threatening.' is not an exaggeration.

Effective communication is crucial for successful learning, and this involves much more than just issuing orders and expecting your cat to comply. Rather than attempting to bend your cat to your will, your initial focus should be to understand why he's behaving in a certain way. As you gain more knowledge about your cat's needs, you'll discover that nearly every type of behaviour has an explanation and even the most unusual actions can typically be classified into one of three categories. It's important to note that none of these categories is the cat's fault:

1. While a cat's behaviour may be considered 'natural' in the sense that he is following his instincts, sometimes your gentle intervention is necessary to make a situation more tolerable. For instance, cats have a different sleep-wake cycle than humans, and your cat may enter hunting mode and run around the house at night, disrupting your sleep. It might sound like he's dragging a sack full of rocks up and down the stairs! To discourage this nocturnal

mayhem you could try increasing your cat's daytime activity levels with more playtime and interactive toys.

2. Your cat's behaviour is a logical and natural response to a dysfunctional environment. For instance, if he keeps spraying on the sofa instead of using the litter box, you need to identify the issue with the litter box. It could be too big, too small or in the wrong location (too noisy, lacking privacy, or not easily accessible). Perhaps it's not being kept clean or you're using the wrong kind of litter (most cats prefer fine-grained, unscented litter). If you have multiple cats, it's recommended to provide one litter box per cat, plus an additional one.

3. If your cat is exhibiting unusual or problematic behaviour such as avoiding the litter tray, it's a sign that he may feel threatened by something in his environment, such as the presence of an aggressive new cat in the neighbourhood which is causing him anxiety. Alternatively, it could be an indication of an underlying medical issue, in which case you should promptly schedule a visit to the vet.

In addition to avoiding problem behaviour, training a cat can be useful throughout his life. There will be situations where you need to intervene and teach your cat new skills, such as feeling safe and comfortable in a cat carrier for trips to the vet, taking medication, being groomed, or adapting to changes like the introduction of a new pet or baby in the household.

I'M FEELING
GRUMPY

CATS CAN DISPLAY A WIDE RANGE OF BEHAVIOURS
WHEN THEY'RE FEELING GRUMPY. WHILE THERE
MAY BE SOME TRUTH IN THE ASSERTION THAT
SOME CATS ARE TEMPERAMENTALLY GRUMPIER
THAN OTHERS, YOU SHOULD ALWAYS STRIVE TO
UNDERSTAND THE ROOT CAUSES. CHECK THAT
YOU ARE MEETING ALL YOUR CAT'S NEEDS BEFORE
LAZILY DISMISSING HIM AS A SOUR PUSS.

WHAT IS MY CAT REALLY THINKING?

As Jackson Galaxy is eager to point out in his book, *Total Cat Mojo*, 'Grumpy cats are not necessarily unhappy cats. They just have a lower tolerance for the things that annoy them. If you can figure out what those things are and help them avoid them, you'll have a happier cat.'

Some signs that your cat might be feeling grumpy include hiding or seeking out solitude to avoid interaction with people or other pets. He will commonly be less inclined to tolerate being petted or cuddled. He might become easily irritated and may react negatively to things that wouldn't usually bother him. A grumpy cat may become more aggressive and display territorial behaviour and lash out or scratch more than usual. Loss of appetite could be a sign of illness, but if your cat is feeling grumpy, he may show less interest in food than usual and he may be less active and appear to have less energy.

You can also learn a lot about your cat's emotional state by paying close attention to his vocalisations. Susanne Schotz is a Swedish phonetics researcher and author who has studied the vocalizations of cats. In her book, *The Secret Language of Cats*, she explains: 'Grumpy cats may use different vocalizations than happy cats. They may produce more low-pitched, growling sounds, which can be a sign of irritation or aggression.'

'Grumpy cats are often misunderstood. They may be perceived as aloof or unfriendly, but in reality, they may just be expressing their natural feline behaviour. It's important to respect a cat's boundaries and learn to read their body language so that we can communicate with them in a way that they understand.'

Pam Johnson-Bennett

That said, grumpy cat behaviour can often be caused by fear, anxiety or insecurity – expressed in body language by an arched back, flattened ears and whiskers, and puffed-up tail – so you should look beyond surface behaviour to try to identify the underlying issue/s that may be driving it. By addressing these emotions and helping your cat feel more secure and confident, you can often improve his overall mood and behaviour.

Cat expert, Abigail Tucker highlights the importance of recognizing the emotional needs of cats, but her simplistic analysis and solution may not always work in isolation. She says, 'Grumpy cats are often just cats who are feeling overlooked or misunderstood. They're sensitive creatures who thrive on attention and affection, and when they don't get it, they can become irritable or distant.' Her advice is a great starting point, but if showering your cat with love and attention doesn't fix the problem, check that you are meeting all his other material and instinctual needs.

If your cat's normal disposition has changed from friendly to irritable, then this is almost certainly caused by a change in his familiar environment or daily routine. Abrupt changes in the household or cat's schedule, no matter how seemingly insignificant, can cause confusion and irritability. Even minor environmental changes, such as moving the furniture, can unsettle some cats. The addition of a new pet or family member can cause anxiety and confusion, and major changes such as moving house can trigger ongoing stress.

'Cats can be moody creatures and may sometimes seem grumpy, but it's important to remember that they have their own personalities and ways of communicating. If your cat is displaying unusual or persistent grumpiness, it's worth checking for any underlying health issues and consulting with your veterinarian.'

Claire Bessant, Chief Executive
of the Feline Advisory Bureau

I'M
BORED

CATS ARE CURIOUS AND PLAYFUL ANIMALS,
BUT THEY CAN ALSO BECOME BORED EASILY.
REMEMBER, IT'S YOUR RESPONSIBILITY TO PROVIDE
YOUR CAT WITH A STIMULATING ENVIRONMENT
THAT MEETS HIS DAILY NEED TO HUNT, CATCH,
KILL, EAT, GROOM, SLEEP (HCKEGS).

Here are some signs that your cat may be bored:

- **EXCESSIVE SLEEPING:** while cats do sleep a lot, if you notice your cat sleeping more than usual, it could be a sign of boredom.

- **EXCESSIVE GROOMING:** if your cat is grooming themselves excessively, it could be a sign of boredom.

- **HIDING OR AVOIDING INTERACTION:** if your cat is hiding or avoiding interaction with you or other pets in the household, it could be a sign that they are not getting enough stimulation.

- **DESTRUCTIVE BEHAVIOUR:** if your cat starts to scratch furniture, chew on plants or household items, or knock things over, it could be a sign of boredom and frustration.

- **ATTENTION-SEEKING BEHAVIOUR:** if your cat is constantly meowing or pawing at you for attention, it could be a sign that they are bored and looking for ways to interact with you.

- **WEIGHT GAIN** due to a lack of physical activity, play, and mental stimulation.

If you notice any of these signs, you probably need to find ways to provide your cat with more stimulation and playtime. The latter three responses to boredom – destruction, attention-seeking and weight gain – are most likely to spur a lazy owner into action but the first three – sleeping, grooming and hiding – are the most easily ignored.

However, even if your cat doesn't make his problem your problem, this doesn't lessen your responsibility to help him. A bored cat is an unhappy cat; an unhappy cat will eventually become an unhealthy cat and finally, an ill cat, So, if your cat is bored, make positive lasting changes today.

'If your cat is bored, they may develop some bad habits or even start doing things that are either unhealthy for them or frustrating for you. Repetitive behaviours, overeating, terrorizing other pets, or even becoming destructive are all potential signs that your cat is bored.'

Kristen Levine

Boredom isn't such an issue for outdoor cats. Whenever they get restless, they can always go on a territorial recce or a hunting trip if you aren't providing enough stimulation at home. However, indoor cats don't have the same opportunities for play and exploration. They rely on you to provide all their behavioural, emotional and environmental needs.

If you have an indoor cat, Jackson Galaxy offers an ingenious way to enrich your cat's environment to compensate for his inability to hunt and patrol his territory outdoors. In his book *Total Cat Mojo*, Galaxy suggests creating a 'Catio' which he describes as 'a space that you can make for cats (which of course you can share with them) by enclosing your existing patio or creating an enclosure. There you can offer great vertical spaces, wooden objects that they can scratch on, different grasses, including catnip ... even hunting that can happen when critters make their way inside.'

As previously suggested, it's very beneficial to add vertical spaces throughout your home and to be aware of how your cat gets around the house (from sofa to cupboard, cupboard to curtains, etc.). This means you can design an environment that is ergonomic for your cat without being antisocial, keeping some places off-limits (e.g., curtains, kitchen counters, on top of the television) and not have to spend half your time bending over to pick up things that your cat has knocked off surfaces as he patrols around his indoor kingdom.

Even if your cat can't go outdoors, it's a good idea to create a window perch or seat for your cat so that he can see what's going on outside. You might feel that it is cruel to show him what he can't have, but he won't see it that way. He'll be able to spend hours chattering at the birds and being distracted by their every little movement. You can also create interesting play challenges around the house for when you're away, such as a puzzle feeder that requires him to use his problem-solving skills to earn a food reward, or a pole-type dangling toy for safe hunting play.

If your cat lies in ambush and then
attacks your ankles, it's another sign
that he needs more interactive playtime. It doesn't mean
he hates you; he's just bored and frustrated. Increase
your interactive hunting play time and then reduce the
opportunities for your cat to hide in his favourite ankle-level
ambush spots by making them inaccessible or placing a
motion-activated cat deterrent there. Avoid punishing your
cat for this unwanted
behaviour, as it will
only make him
more anxious and
aggressive.

Instead of buying more
toys, try rotating the ones
you have. Put most of
them away and bring them
out again later to renew
his interest. You can also
make objects more interesting
by setting them up in a unique way.
For example, a ball can become a
fascinating challenge when it's tucked
inside a cereal packet or cardboard
tube. With a little creativity, you can
easily entertain your cat and satisfy
his hunting instincts.

I'M
DEPRESSED

CAT DEPRESSION SYMPTOMS ARE VERY SIMILAR TO
THOSE IN PEOPLE. A DEPRESSED CAT WILL EXHIBIT
LOW ENERGY LEVELS, LOSS OF APPETITE, NEGLECT
OF FAVOURITE ACTIVITIES OR TOYS, CHANGES
IN SLEEP PATTERNS, SPRAYING OR CHANGES IN
BATHROOM HABITS, EXCESSIVE SCRATCHING, POOR
OR EXCESSIVE GROOMING, WITHDRAWAL FROM
SOCIAL INTERACTIONS WITH PEOPLE OR OTHER PETS,
MEOWING MORE OR LESS THAN USUAL OR MAKING
LOW-PITCHED, MOURNFUL MEOWS AND SHOW
INCREASED IRRITABILITY OR AGGRESSION.

Most biologists now recognise that animals experience
emotions, which are not simply the result of some bodily
state that leads to an action. Marc Bekoff, an ethologist and
author who specializes in animal behaviour, sums up the
scientific consensus: 'Non-human animals have emotions

76

and are capable of exhibiting them. They can be happy, sad, frustrated, angry, and many other emotions that we associate with human beings.'

In fact, a recent survey of an admittedly small sample of one thousand dogs conducted in the UK by the charity Guide Dogs, reported that nearly three-quarters were showing signs of poor mental health. There haven't been any large-scale surveys specifically focused on the prevalence of depression in cats, but several studies suggest that cats can experience depression-like symptoms.

One study published in the *Journal of Veterinary Behavior* found that cats who experienced changes in their environment, such as moving to a new home or the arrival of a new pet, were more likely to exhibit behaviours associated with depression. These include decreased appetite and decreased grooming. Another study published in *PLOS ONE* found that cats who were housed in small cages without any environmental enrichment showed signs of decreased activity and altered behaviours, which the researchers interpreted as possible signs of depression.

Depression in cats is linked to the same chemical deficiencies in the brain as in humans, including a lack of the neurotransmitter serotonin. Environmental conditions such as bereavement or separation, moving house, a new baby or pet, trauma from illness, injury or abuse such as violence or long periods of isolation, can all cause depression in cats. The two most common triggers are the loss of a companion animal or the loss of an owner.

Unsurprisingly, in response to the scientific community's belated recognition of the emotional lives of our beloved pets, medicating cats for depression has become big business. Huge pharmaceutical companies have even established their own pets division which earns the company over a billion dollars each year. Anti-depressants for cats and dogs are a lucrative growing part of this revenue.

However, if your cat is exhibiting the symptoms of depression, once a vet has ruled out a medical cause, there are lots of social interventions which you can use before resorting to medication. The key is early diagnosis: the quicker you identify that there is a problem, the shorter the opportunity for the problem to become entrenched.

Fortunately, as with humans, certain behavioural treatments such as increased exercise, play and social interaction are very effective at combating depression. You might also consider adding another cat to your family to increase social support and companionship. It isn't rocket science: John Ciribassi, past president of the American Veterinary Society of Animal Behaviour advises: 'Keep them engaged, do more of the things they like to do, get them a little more exercise, and they should be fine'.

I'M TOO
HOT

THE NORMAL BODY TEMPERATURE RANGE FOR A CAT IS BETWEEN 99.5°F AND 102.5°F. CATS SHOULD AVOID CONDITIONS EXCEEDING 100°F (38°C) AS IT CAN BECOME TOO HOT FOR THEM. ALTHOUGH CATS ENJOY WARMTH, THEY ARE STILL SUSCEPTIBLE TO OVERHEATING.

WHAT IS MY CAT REALLY THINKING?

It may come as a surprise, but cats (and dogs) are at a greater risk of suffering from heat exhaustion and stroke compared to humans. This is due to their basic physiology, which includes a higher metabolic rate, smaller body area, limited ability to sweat, fur coat, etc.

Their bodies have a difficult time regulating internal temperature because they primarily cool themselves down by panting and through the sweat glands located on their paw pads. These sweat glands are not very effective at regulating body temperature and are mainly used for marking territory. Even so, whenever your cat's feet feel clammy with sweat, it's a warning sign that he is getting warm.

Despite this, heat stroke in cats remains rare. If your cat shows signs of being overheated – including restlessness, sweating, panting, drooling, breathing rapidly, racing pulse, glazed eyes, red tongue, mouth and gums, vomiting,

lethargy, stumbling or staggering – take him to a cool place, offer him plenty of cool, fresh water and damp his fur with a wet cloth or spray his fur with cool water using a mister and train a large fan on him.

> 'Signs of heatstroke include panting, mental dullness, bruising and seizures … Unlike dogs, panting is always an emergency in cats.'
>
> Dr Bridget Lyons

On a hot day, even an indoor environment without air conditioning can pose an overheating risk for your cat. A lack of air circulation in a closed interior space can cause your pet's temperature to rise quickly. Cool your home by opening windows, closing curtains and using fans to circulate the air.

Along with open windows, fans, and any form of air conditioning you may have, it is essential to ensure your cat has access to plenty of fresh drinking water to prevent dehydration. Check your cat's body temperature using an ear thermometer. If it is higher than 104°F, it can be a sign of heatstroke or illness. If you have any concerns, contact your veterinarian as soon as you notice any signs of heat-related illness or dehydration. Your cat may need intravenous fluids or another treatment urgently to combat the symptoms.

WHAT IS MY CAT REALLY THINKING?

Cats are at increased risk of overheating if they fall into one or more of these categories: obese, pregnant, kitten, old cat, flat-faced breed (e.g., Persians, Himalayans), long-haired or after excessive exercise.

Regardless of the temperature, under no circumstances should you leave your cat or any other pet unattended in a car, not even for a moment with the windows open. When it is a mere 22°C outside, your cat can fatally overheat in as little as ten minutes and the temperature inside a car can reach an unbearable 47°C within less than an hour. Other factors to consider during hot weather:

- Don't let your cat out during the hottest hours of the day.

- Double-check inside sheds and greenhouses before you close their doors, to ensure your cat doesn't get locked inside.

- Keep several bowls of fresh, cool drinking water around the house and garden and replace the water regularly.

- Brush your cat more often to remove his undercoat. Don't be tempted to shave the fur completely, since it provides some protection from the sun's harmful ultraviolet rays.

I'M TOO
COLD

THE NORMAL BODY TEMPERATURE RANGE FOR A
CAT IS BETWEEN 99.5°F AND 102.5°F. IF YOUR CAT'S
TEMPERATURE DROPS BELOW 99°F, HE MAY BE PRONE
TO MILD HYPOTHERMIA. HOWEVER, YOU CAN TAKE
SIMPLE MEASURES TO ENSURE YOUR CAT STAYS COSY
DURING THE COLDEST MONTHS AND MAINTAINS A
COMFORTABLE BODY TEMPERATURE.

83

WHAT IS MY CAT REALLY THINKING?

To detect if your cat is feeling cold, you'll need to pay extra attention since cats tend to conceal their discomfort and may hide themselves away. Here are some subtle signs that your cat may be cold:

1. COOL EXTREMITIES: his ears, paws and the tip of his tail lose heat first. If these body parts feel cold, your cat may be uncomfortably chilly.

2. RESTING ON DIRECT HEAT SOURCES: if you notice your cat frequently lounging on a radiator or other warm spots, he's trying to increase his body temperature.

3. The degree to which your cat is curled up is also an indicator of his temperature. As the temperature drops, he will lower his head, pull in his feet and curl up his body to keep warm. By the time the temperature reaches 55°F, he may even use his tail to cover half of his face, hiding his feet from view.

4. CURLING INTO A BALL: while this could be a typical sleeping position for your cat, it could also indicate he is feeling very cold. A chilly cat will tuck his paws and tail beneath his body to conserve heat.

5. SEEKING CUDDLES: if your cat persistently wants to snuggle with you, he may be trying to warm himself up. If you have several cats, they will often huddle together for warmth.

If you observe any of these symptoms, phone your vet immediately:

- Signs of mild hypothermia (body temperature of 90-99°F) in cats include weakness, shivering, lack of mental alertness.

- Signs of moderate hypothermia (82-90°F) include muscle stiffness, low blood pressure, unresponsive, stupor-like state, slow, shallow breathing.

- Signs of severe hypothermia (less than 82°F) include fixed and dilated pupils, inaudible heartbeat, difficulty breathing.

'Keeping cats warm is especially important for kittens, older cats, and cats with medical conditions. You can use a heated cat bed, make sure their sleeping area is warm and draft-free, and dress them in a sweater or coat. Keeping cats warm helps them conserve energy and stay healthy.'

Dr Jennifer Coates, veterinarian and author

There are several ways to warm up your cat:

- Ensure that your home is properly insulated and heated during cold weather. This will help keep your cat warm and comfortable. If you can't afford/don't want to heat the whole house, set up a comfortable bed for your cat in a warm and draft-free area of your home. You can also add a soft blanket or heated cat bed to create a toasty spot for your cat to snuggle up in.

- Use a heating pad: switch to a low setting and cover it with a towel or blanket. Place it in your cat's bed, but make sure it's not too hot, and always supervise your cat when using a heating pad.

- Layer up: consider getting your cat a sweater or coat to wear during the colder months. Make sure it fits well and doesn't restrict his movement.

- Play with him more regularly. Increased activity will raise his body temperature and stimulate him in a positive way.

- Cuddle with your cat: spending some quality time snuggling with your cat on the sofa or in bed can also help warm him up, plus it's a great way to bond and keep yourself warm.

Here are some other factors to consider around the home to keep your cat safe during cold weather:

- KEEP HIM INDOORS: the best way to keep your cat safe during extreme cold weather is to keep him inside the house.

- CAT FLAPS: if your cat has access to the outdoors, make sure he can come back inside through the cat flap. Check it regularly during cold weather to ensure it's not frozen shut by snow or ice.

- ROAD GRIT: rock salt used to grit roads and pavements can cause dehydration, pancreatitis and liver failure if ingested by your cat. Consider purchasing booties for your cat to wear or wipe his paws with a warm damp cloth after he come indoors. During snowy and icy weather, try to keep your cat away from areas where salt has been used or wash his paws when he returns home. Symptoms of rock salt ingestion, such as burns to the mouth and throat, excessive salivating and drinking, require immediate veterinary attention.

- ENSURE ACCESS TO FRESH WATER: keep your cat's water bowl filled with fresh water and check it regularly to ensure it has not frozen over. Incidentally, if you ever observe your cat dipping his paw into his water bowl and then licking his paw, it's a sign that the bowl is in the wrong place and that he doesn't feel safe enough to place his head in the bowl. If this is the case, move the bowl to a quieter and more private location.

- ACTIVELY MONITOR HIS BEHAVIOUR: keep a close eye on him during cold weather. If he shows signs of shivering, lethargy or disorientation, weakness, slow breathing, bring him indoors immediately and contact your veterinarian.

I'M IN PAIN /
FEELING ILL

EVEN THOUGH CATS CAN ATTRACT OUR
ATTENTION IN A NUMBER OF WAYS, VOCALLY
AND PHYSICALLY, THEY HAVE A TENDENCY TO
CONCEAL OR TOLERATE ILLNESS. SO, YOUR CAT'S
WELL-BEING IS IN YOUR HANDS. REMAIN VIGILANT
TO PHYSICAL SYMPTOMS AND BEHAVIOURAL
CHANGES THAT COULD INDICATE SICKNESS. YOU
KNOW YOUR CAT BETTER THAN ANYONE ELSE,
SO IF YOU HAVE ANY CONCERNS ABOUT YOUR
CAT'S HEALTH, CONTACT YOUR VETERINARIAN,
NO MATTER HOW TRIVIAL YOUR WORRIES.

Veterinarian Dr Karen Becker explains why cats conceal
their pain: 'Cats are experts at hiding illness. In nature,
showing weakness makes them more vulnerable to
predators. And at home, despite their ability to verbalize
discomfort, cats prefer to suffer in silence.'

Veterinary hospital manager Jenna Stregowski offers another explanation for why cats and many other animals live with pain: 'They simply do not have an emotional relationship with their discomfort. Animals tend to accept the pain or illness as the new normal and move on. It may not be until they are extremely ill that their sickness becomes obvious to humans.'

The best way to tell if your cat is ill is by noticing subtle changes in behaviour, however small. *Feline Behaviour Guidelines* issued by The American Association of Feline Practitioners, advises: 'In cats, physical illness and pain are most often recognized on the basis of a *non-specific change in behaviour*'. Your cat may be more subdued than normal, sit in a hunched position, carry her head and tail in a different way, hide away and have stiff body movements, be unwilling to move or display uncharacteristic aggression.

A change in grooming routine is a dead giveaway that something is wrong. A cat in discomfort often stops grooming, leading to a messy dull or greasy coat with mats. Excessive grooming (leading to bald spots, irritated skin, and rashes) can also indicate a problem, e.g., allergies or parasites such as fleas, mites or ringworm.

89

THE TOP 16 SIGNS THAT YOUR CAT MAY BE ILL

1. Behavioural changes, especially hiding away.

2. Appetite change (has not eaten properly for 24 hours), unexplained weight loss or gain.

3. Litter box issues.

4. General lethargy, reduction in energy/activity level, lack of interest.

5. Frequent vomiting or change in bowel movements.

6. Blood in urine, stool, or vomit.

7. Diarrhoea or constipation.

8. Excessive drinking or urination.

9. Lameness or stiffness.

10. Bad breath, drooling, panting.

11. Skin complaints, hair loss, sores, lumps.

12. Coughing, sneezing, laboured breathing.

13. Dry, red, or cloudy eyes.

14. Discharges from eyes or nose.

15. Change in gum colour from usual healthy deep pink.

16. Dehydration: gently grip his skin near his shoulder blades, pull it up and away from his, then let go. If he is well hydrated, the skin should snap back into place immediately.

FLEA AND WORM TREATMENT: The symptoms mentioned above indicate an underlying illness. However, one of the most important health issues that is often neglected by pet owners is routine flea and worm treatment that eliminates fleas and worms while ensuring a cat's long-term protection. Flea and worm treatments are crucial for your cat as they effectively eradicate these parasites and disrupt their life cycle, preventing their spread and keeping your pet under control.

Kittens are particularly vulnerable to flea infestations and anaemia caused by blood loss. Worms live in the intestines, where they can damage the gut lining and eat food that should be digested by the cat. While adult cats generally experience milder effects from worm infestations, they can severely impact the health of kittens.

Treatments are available in various forms such as liquids, granules, collars, tablets and spot-ons, which are liquid treatments applied to directly to the cat's skin. The choice of medication depends on your pet's preferences and their ease of medication intake. Spot-on treatments are popular due to their convenient application and rapid activation. Ask your vet for advice.

'Cats that are ill will usually show changes in overall appearance, energy level, sociability, coat appearance and/or amount of shedding, appetite, litterbox usage, breathing, or discharges from the eyes or nose. In general, any sudden change should alert you that your cat needs veterinary attention.'

Tammy Hunter

POISONING: Dozens of house and garden plants are poisonous to cats, as well as many foods as well as other common hazards around the home such as milk (most cats are lactose intolerant and dairy milk will upset their stomach), chocolate, grapes, raisins, onions, garlic, chives, leeks, avocado, alcohol, coffee beans, raw dough, dog food, blue cheese, macadamia nuts, xylitol (artificial sweetener found in sugar-free gum, bread and other baked goods), raw meat, almonds, walnuts, pistachios, pecans, Niger bird seeds, slug pellets, human drugs (and anything mouldy, so keep your cat away from your food waste bin).

The symptoms of poisoning can vary depending on the type and amount of the poisonous substance ingested. These symptoms may include agitation, drooling, panting, nausea, vomiting, diarrhoea, oral irritation, pale gums, heart issues, excessive bruising or bleeding, unsteadiness on feet, drowsiness, breathing problems, tremors and convulsions. If you suspect that your cat has ingested something toxic, it's crucial to seek immediate veterinary treatment.

I'M IN HEAT

AT AROUND FOUR MONTHS OLD, CATS REACH SEXUAL MATURITY AND CAN START BREEDING. IT CAN BE A HAIR-RAISING EXPERIENCE FOR OWNERS WHEN THEIR FEMALE CAT GOES INTO HEAT FOR THE FIRST TIME BECAUSE PERSONALITY CHANGES OVERNIGHT IN RESPONSE TO THE HORMONE CHANGES IN HER BODY.

However, she doesn't do this once or twice a year – once it starts, she will go into heat for about six days every two or three weeks until either she gets pregnant or gets spayed.

There are several signs that indicate your cat is in heat:

- Extreme vocalizing with low insistent yowling – caterwauling – that may sound like pain – don't worry, this is natural. She is calling out for a mate.

- Restlessness; your cat can't settle. She paces around and stares out of the window. longingly, desperate to go outside and find a mate.

- Flirtatious and extra-affectionate behaviour towards humans.

- Rolling on the floor and rubbing against everything! It seems she can't pass by anything without rubbing her scent onto it to attract a male cat. This includes you.

- Raised hindquarters, arching of the back and swishing her tail from side to side – these actions spread pheromones and send a clear visual signal to male cats that she is ready to mate.

- Assuming the mating position – pressing her front elbows against the floor whilst crouching with her back legs, buttocks raised into the air, tail held to the side to expose her genitals. She may also knead the floor with her back feet at the same time (which is thought to help ovulation).

- Spraying; yes, female cats can spray too – it's yet another way of spreading pheromones to attract a mate. (If she isn't in heat, it may be a sign that she has a UTI.)

- During this time, your cat's genital area may become swollen and uncomfortable, causing her to spend more time grooming that area. You may even notice a clear, watery discharge.

'The increased vocalization is the hallmark sign of a heat cycle in a cat. This is a natural signal showing the cat is calling out for a mate. Owners sometimes think this is a sign of pain when in reality, it's simply biology.'

Jim D Carlson

To keep your cat calm during her heat cycle, isolate her from male cats by keeping doors and windows closed and curtains drawn. If she can see male cats outside, she will become highly motivated to try to escape from the house.

'How do I shut my cat up when they're in heat? The bottom line is you can't. You can't stop nature from doing what nature does. The only way to stop the caterwauling is for your cat not to be in heat in the first place.'

Jackson Galaxy

Offer her plenty of attention and physical contact through petting, cuddling and brushing. Extra playtime can also help distract her from restlessness. Ensure her litter box is clean and odour-free to encourage her to mark it instead of other parts of the house (avoiding ammonia-based cleaners which may encourage your cat to spray more). Providing warmth with a warm towel or heat pack can also help. Some cats may respond well to soothing music (smooth jazz or classical – experiment!), catnip or herbal remedies (consult a vet first). Pheromone products may also help with anxiety-related behaviours, but it's unclear whether they are effective for cats in heat.

If you have a female kitten and you're unsure about what to expect, it's best to consult with your veterinarian to discuss your cat's cycle and the option of neutering. To prevent unwanted pregnancies, most vets recommend spaying female cats at four to five months of age. This offers various benefits, such as the removal of ovaries and uterus to prevent the risk of serious uterine infection called pyometra. It also reduces the risk of mammary tumours.

Additionally, neutering helps to control the cat population by minimizing the number of unwanted kittens and eliminating male cats' territorial behaviour such as fighting, urine spraying, and screaming. Overall, neutering is highly beneficial for both the cat and its owner.

OH NO, NOT
CHILDREN

WHILST MANY DOGS ARE VERY PATIENT AND
LONG-SUFFERING IN THE COMPANY OF CHILDREN,
MOST CATS DO NOT RESPOND WELL TO INCREASED
NOISE LEVELS AND UNPREDICTABLE ENERGY. CATS
WILL NATURALLY GRAVITATE TOWARDS THE QUIETEST,
STILLEST PERSON IN A ROOM, WHICH IS WHY PEOPLE
WHO DON'T LIKE CATS OFTEN FIND THEMSELVES
WITH A CAT IN THEIR LAP, PRECISELY BECAUSE THEY
IGNORED IT AND TRIED TO APPEAR INVISIBLE.

Sadly, one of the main reasons that cats end up in animal shelters or get rehomed is that their owners do not believe they can be trusted to be safe around children. Some expectant parents even rehome their cat before their baby has been born, which is unfortunate because there is no better opportunity to learn empathy and respect for animals than growing up in a household with pets.

If you want to learn how to manage your household – and crucially, your cat's environment – so that felines and children can live in peace and harmony, you should read Jackson Galaxy's book, *Total Cat Mojo* in which he offers comprehensive advice for successfully bringing a cat into a child's home, or vice versa.

One of the foundations of Jackson Galaxy's approach to cat behaviour and welfare is what he calls the 'Three Rs' which stand for 'Routines, Rituals and Rhythm.' He explains: 'Every home has its natural rise-and-fall energy cycles … As you begin to establish rituals and routines with your cat, and base them on your home's energy spikes, you create a rhythm … But it's not just about getting your cat to conform to your rhythm. It's about folding their needs and yours into a *household* rhythm.'

Once you realise that cleaning the litterbox, playing with, and cuddling your cat are as important as making dinner or dropping your kids off to school, you will instinctively find solutions to new situations that keep both your family and cat nurtured, safe and happy. This doesn't mean making either the centre of attention, but understanding that all their distinct needs flow together. Neither does this mean treating your cat like a human. Quite the opposite: your cat has very different needs from other members of the household.

For example, expectant parents decorating a nursery in preparation for a new baby might decide to banish the cat from the room, to keep cat and baby apart. But a better solution is counterintuitive – instead of taking away some of your cat's territory and filling a room with new things that don't smell of her (which is guaranteed to stress her out) it's preferable to involve her fully so that she can see the crib and rub against it. Provide her with elevated space in the nursery, so that she can climb high and watch the comings and goings from a safe vantage point. Jackson Galaxy even recommends feeding the cat in the nursery and playing recordings of crying babies to desensitize her and to build positive associations with the arrival of the new baby.

The other misguided instinct of new parents is to childproof the home, which includes the cat's belongings, such as litter trays, which might get moved into 'territorial exile' such as the garage or some other place that causes major disturbance to the cat. A simpler, cat-focused solution which benefits everyone is to empty the litter tray regularly and distract your child/ren by giving them more interesting things to play with.

> 'Cats and young children can absolutely live safely and happily together if you adopt a cat with the right temperament. The best cats for kids are gentle, friendly and patient. While rumour has it that many cats are cranky, most can make loving pets.'
>
> Christine O'Brien

Creating harmony between cats and children requires the willingness to make hard choices that can often be counterintuitive. Here's a starter list of do's and don'ts:

1. Used a stuffed animal to teach your children how to hold and handle a cat – gentle petting, no pulling of tails and ears.

2. Show your children where cats like to be petted (e.g., on their cheeks) and which areas to avoid (e.g., on their belly or head-to-toe stroking).

3. One-finger petting or petting with an open hand are recommended.

4. Model good behaviour towards your cat and they will copy you.

5. Teach children to talk softly and gently to and around the cat. No yelling or screaming allowed.

6. Keep play sessions with cat and children short. Kittens need to sleep a lot.

7. Always refer to the cat by name or he/she and never 'it' and encourage your children to do the same. Your cat is not an object; she is a living thing with individual emotions, and she will learn from any disrespectful or cruel behaviour very quickly.

8. Respect the cat's personal space. You cannot force her to pay you attention.

9. Don't disturb her when she is eating, sleeping or using the litterbox.

10. Teach your children about your cat's body language, so that if she swishes her tail, pins back her ears or her eyes grow wide, they understand that she's not feeling sociable. This knowledge can prevent escalation to your cat growling, scratching or biting.

11. Teach your children to care for your cat by giving them age-appropriate cat-related responsibilities, such as feeding, providing fresh water, emptying the litter tray. Emphasize that this is an important way to show their love for the cat.

12. Never leave cats and children together unsupervised.

I NEED SOME
ME TIME

CATS TYPICALLY HAVE SPECIFIC SPOTS IN THEIR HOMES WHERE THEY FEEL SECURE AND PREFER NOT TO BE BOTHERED. IT'S CRUCIAL TO RESPECT THEIR PRIVACY AND REFRAIN FROM DISTURBING THEM WHILE THEY'RE IN THEIR DESIGNATED SAFE AREA. ALLOWING THEM TO DO AS THEY PLEASE (USUALLY DOZING) IN THEIR SANCTUARY IS IMPORTANT, AND IT'S ADVISABLE TO DISCOURAGE FAMILY MEMBERS FROM DISRUPTING THEIR PEACE. IN A HOUSEHOLD WITH MORE THAN ONE CAT, IT'S EVEN MORE CRUCIAL TO PROVIDE EACH FELINE WITH THEIR OWN PRIVATE SPACE.

'Cats have a scam going – you buy the food, they eat the food, they go away; that's the deal.'

Eddie Izzard

According to John Alderton, author of *Understanding Your Cat*, 'A cat's breed affects the kind of companionship that it prefers'. In *The Cat Whisperer*, Claire Bessant claims that a researcher in the US 'has recognised two different types of feline character within the groups of kittens she has studied … excitable and nervous, and those which are much more relaxed and quiet in their attitude to life and its challenges'.

She discusses a similar pattern in adult cats: 'Current work on the personality of the adult cat … points to the likelihood of there being two different and distinct types.' She describes type one as needing 'lots of social contact with both people and other cats and is relaxed in their company.' The second type 'seems only to enjoy the company of one or two members of its human family … and often doesn't form bonds with other cats either.'

If you have a type two cat, you may notice that the more you try to cuddle her and shower her with affection, the less interest she shows in you. She typically won't seek attention and may even ignore visitors. If you own such a cat, don't blame yourself for her standoffish behaviour. She may have been born that way. Bessant concludes that more research

needs to be done to discover the
extent to which nature and
nurture have produced these
two types.

Research on feline
personalities and
behaviour is an active
field of study. For
example, a study
published in the *Journal
of Veterinary Behavior*
in 2017 identified three
feline personality dimensions:
skittishness, outgoingness and
dominance. Another published a year earlier
in the journal *PLOS ONE* recognises five feline
personality traits: neuroticism, extraversion, dominance,
impulsiveness and agreeableness.

Despite all this, the happiness of your cat is highly impacted
by your actions and the type of lifestyle you provide for her.
Since cats are territorial animals, their surroundings play a
crucial role. Creating a cat-friendly home requires certain
compromises that benefit you and your feline companion,
ensuring that the environment is suitable for both of you.
Regardless of your cat's innate personality, rest assured
that your cat's behaviour will most certainly be influenced
by your diligent and unstinting care, compassion and

willingness to see the world from her point of view. Most importantly, the physical environment and positive routines you maintain for her, as well as the day-to-day atmosphere in your home will always remain the major contributing factors to her wellbeing.

'They really are affectionate towards their owners but it's not their first priority – it's physical space. It's part of being a cat and it comes from their ancestors thousands of years ago.'

John Bradshaw

Cats tend to snooze for around 18 hours a day to replenish the energy they consume while hunting, playing and exploring their environment. Instead of having one continuous sleep cycle during the night like humans, they prefer to have multiple naps throughout the day. Allowing your cat to snuggle with you at night could alleviate anxiety and help you get to sleep, but don't forget that, unlike dogs, cats don't sleep soundly all night long. So, when your cat starts wandering in the early hours or swiping at your face at dawn, please be forgiving – it's her nature.

WAKE UP!

MANY CAT OWNERS FIND THEMSELVES FRUSTRATED WITH THEIR FURRY COMPANIONS CRYING LOUDLY AND PERSISTENTLY DURING THE NIGHT. THIS BEHAVIOUR IS QUITE COMMON AMONG OLDER CATS, BUT IT CAN ALSO HAPPEN TO CATS OF ANY AGE, ESPECIALLY IF THEY LEARN THAT CRYING CAN GET THEM WHAT THEY WANT, SUCH AS FOOD OR ATTENTION. TRY TO FIGURE OUT THE UNDERLYING CAUSE RATHER THAN SIMPLY TRYING TO SILENCE IT.

Kittens use meowing to communicate with their mothers, signalling that they are hungry, cold, scared, or lonely. As they grow older, they develop a repertoire of about a hundred vocalizations that they use to communicate with other cats, including hissing, growling, trilling, and chattering. However, adult cats rarely meow at each other, reserving this form of communication for humans. This is because we often fail to understand their more nuanced sounds and misinterpret their subtle body language.

'Cats are like babies, you have to learn to read their moods and anticipate their needs. They can be noisy and restless at night, but with patience and understanding, they become your most loyal companion.'

Andrea Jordan

There are various reasons why cats may meow during the night, including a need for attention, reassurance, or boredom. The most likely cause is inadequate daytime stimulation and exercise. This issue is more common among indoor cats who don't have the freedom to play, hunt, or roam outside. As a result, indoor cats may feel bored and restless, especially when left alone for extended periods.

In addition to a lack of exercise and stimulation, there can be other reasons for night-time meowing. For example, cats may meow at night because they are hungry, thirsty,

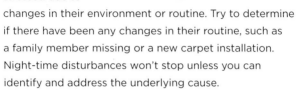

or need to use the litter
box. They may also be
feeling anxious or
stressed due to
changes in their environment or routine. Try to determine
if there have been any changes in their routine, such as
a family member missing or a new carpet installation.
Night-time disturbances won't stop unless you can
identify and address the underlying cause.

Meanwhile, make sure your cat is getting plenty of
stimulation and exercise during the day. As cats are
nocturnal by nature, they are naturally more active at
night. If when they are not able to engage in their natural
behaviours during the day, they may feel compelled to
do so after dark.

To reduce night-time restlessness, consider playing an
active game with your cat before bedtime to tire him out.
You could also play soothing music, such as easy listening,
smooth classical, or talk radio to calm him down. Ignoring
the behaviour is the best way to discourage it, rather than
shushing or shouting at your cat, which only reinforces their
attention-seeking behaviour.

It is also important to establish a regular routine for feeding,
playtime, and sleep, and to stick to this routine as much as
possible. This can help to reduce stress and anxiety for cats
and make them feel more secure and comfortable in their
environment.

PAY ME SOME
ATTENTION!

ALTHOUGH CATS ARE KNOWN FOR THEIR COOL
AND DISTANT DEMEANOUR, THEY OCCASIONALLY
ABANDON THEIR FAÇADE AND CRAVE ATTENTION,
MUCH LIKE A HUMAN TODDLER. IT DOESN'T MATTER
WHAT TIME OF DAY OR NIGHT, OR WHETHER YOU'RE
TRYING TO FIND SOME PRIVACY IN THE BATHROOM,
WHEN A CAT WANTS ATTENTION, EVERYBODY
KNOWS ABOUT IT.

WHAT IS MY CAT REALLY THINKING?

Research has indicated that a cat's vocalizations for food or attention share several acoustic characteristics with the sound of a crying human baby, triggering a biological response in adults. Over thousands of years of interaction between cats and humans, this convergence has become almost inevitable.

> 'Cats are notorious attention-seekers. They want what they want when they want it. And if they don't get it, they can be quite insistent.'
>
> Janet Jackson

Interestingly, scientists have found that cat meows are more generic than most cat owners assume. Although meows are loud to grab attention, cats communicate with their owners with less subtlety than we credit them for.

In a recent study published in the *Journal of Comparative Psychology*, researchers from Cornell University's Department of Psychology asked cat owners to decipher meows from 12 cats in five different behavioural contexts. Although their accuracy was slightly better than chance, it was not significant enough to conclude that cats' meows were specific to certain situations. The researchers concluded that, 'Meows are generalized, somewhat negative stimuli, that capture human attention.' This suggests that humans are surprisingly bad at interpreting any subtleties in a cat's vocalizations, whether real or perceived.

Many cat owners would disagree with the idea that their cats' meows are generic and believe that their cats have specific vocalizations for different situations. However, it's likely that cats have learned to use the meows that elicit the most human response.

Most cat owners would argue against this. They are convinced that their cat has distinct cries for different situations, one meow for 'I want attention,' another for 'I'm hungry!' and another still for 'I'm angry'. It's more likely that the cat has simply learned to use whichever vocalisations provoke a human response; or rather, humans have conditioned themselves to respond to certain sounds by attaching meaning to them and neglecting other sounds by offering no anthropomorphic interpretation.

> 'Cats are the ultimate attention seekers. They have this ability to demand attention whenever they want it.'
>
> Matt Haig

Many cat owners report that their cats make a beeping noise – a quick 'bip' or 'eck' sound, which they interpret as, 'Ahem – excuse me.' When they want attention, cats also perform what can only be described as 'burbling' – a hybrid somewhere between a purr, meow and a growl.

111

If you've ever had to shut your cat in a room against her will (e.g., she's been stealing food and you want to give the other cats a chance to eat undisturbed), then you may be treated to the sound of a cat wailing – the most plaintive of sounds. The wail demands attention while simultaneously ripping your heart out with powerful harmonics that convey timeless themes of loss, betrayal and gross injustice!

As cats age, they may start to wail for various reasons. One possible cause is disorientation due to sensory loss, such as hearing, smell, or sight, or even dementia. Night-time wailing can also be a sign of loneliness, boredom, or confusion, as everyone else is asleep and not providing attention. These excessive vocalizations could also indicate underlying medical conditions.

If you're unsure about the cause of your cat's wailing, consult a vet to rule out any medical issues. An older cat who's used to living with other cats may start wailing when feeling lonely and missing companionship. Additionally, digestion issues can also cause excessive vocalizations, so it's worth discussing with your vet how to address these problems.

By taking care of your older cat's physical and emotional needs, you can help to minimize the chances of wailing and ensure a comfortable life for your beloved pet.

Cats can often be a source of annoyance when you're on the phone, and the more important the call, the more they seem to demand attention. But what is it about talking into a small plastic box that makes them so needy?

The truth is cats don't understand that you're on the phone. They may believe that you're talking to them, and they're attracted to the sounds coming from your mouth and your non-threatening body language. Additionally, cats like predictability, and they know that when the phone rings, you'll be stationary for a few minutes, which is the perfect opportunity for some petting.

Rather than being annoyed by your cat's behaviour during phone calls, you can use it as an opportunity to increase her sense of security and well-being. Give her some attention every time you're on the phone and enjoy her desire to be close to you. By providing her with the predictability and security she craves, you can turn the annoyance into a positive bonding experience.

> 'Cats are natural attention-seekers, but they're also very discerning about who they seek attention from.'
>
> Martha Stewart

HELLO, PLEASE CHECK OUT MY
BACKSIDE

YOU MIGHT NOT REALISE IT, BUT WHEN YOUR CAT STICKS HER BACKSIDE IN YOUR FACE, SHE IS POLITELY EXPRESSING HER TRUST IN YOU. WHILE PRESENTING BACKSIDES HAS YET TO CATCH ON IN HUMAN SOCIETY, IT IS A COMMON WAY FOR CATS TO GREET THEIR FELINE FRIENDS. RAISING THEIR TAILS IS CONSIDERED GOOD MANNERS IN THE FELINE WORLD, AS IT HELPS THEM EXCHANGE INFORMATION THROUGH PHEROMONES.

When cats first meet, they often adopt a posture we call the 'elevator butt,' where they raise their backside in the air, hold their tail straight, and bend their front paws so that their head is close to the ground. This is a friendly gesture, inviting a good sniff to greet one another, like dogs.

> 'There is no creature better at delicate rudeness than a cat.'
>
> Elizabeth Peters

When your cat presents her backside to you, she is sharing information about herself, her location, and her activities. It may not be the most pleasant thing for us humans, but it is an important part of cat communication. By turning her back to you, she's showing that she feels safe and secure in your presence. The area around her tail is vulnerable, and by exposing it to you, she's demonstrating that she's not afraid of being attacked or hurt. Essentially, she's saying, 'I trust you and feel comfortable around you'.

> 'A raised tail signals, "I mean no threat." So, the combination of a raising a tail with offering a butt-sniffing opportunity is the equivalent of a human's enthusiastic hug or a kiss on each cheek in greeting.'
>
> Amy Shojai

According to research, when a cat approaches another with its tail held high, it is more likely to attract rubbing and sniffing from other cats in the colony. If the other cat also raises its tail, the chances of rubbing increase.

When your cat jumps onto your lap and presents her backside, she's also inviting you to rub alongside her. Typically, cats rub against each other's flanks to exchange scents, but since humans use their hands instead of their whole bodies, the cat ends up facing away from us.

Kittens also present their backsides to their mothers, inviting them to groom their lower area. You don't need to go that far, but it's worth noting that cats only present their backsides to those they feel comfortable and safe around.

It's a great chance for you to bond with her by scratching the hard-to-reach spot at the base of her tail. She'll thank you by continuing to scent you with her head, cheeks, and paws, and may even start kneading you with pure pleasure.

> 'Cats seem to go on the principle that it never does any harm to ask for what you want.'
>
> Joseph Wood Krutch

I'LL JUST LEAVE THIS
HERE

EVERY CAT OWNER HAS LIKELY ENCOUNTERED THE
UNSETTLING SIGHT OF THEIR BELOVED PET BRINGING
IN A DEAD ANIMAL, OR WORSE, A LIVE ONE. IT'S NOT
UNCOMMON FOR CATS TO EXHIBIT THIS BEHAVIOUR,
AND IT'S NOT NECESSARILY A SIGN THAT
THEY'RE NOT BEING FED ENOUGH.

Cats have been natural hunters for thousands of years, and even though they have been domesticated for a relatively short time, they haven't lost their instinct for catching prey. Even though the diets of domestic cats are well-balanced and nutritious, their hunting skills have not been selectively bred out of them. Additionally, cats are capable of digesting raw meat without issue, so it's not harmful to them if they eat what they catch.

This behaviour is most common in spayed female cats. Female cats will often bring back animals to teach their kittens how to eat and hunt, and when they bring these gifts to their owners, they are essentially sharing their expertise. The cat sees their owner as a pupil, and themselves as a teacher, rather than simply trying to show affection.

> 'Many assume the outdoor cat who "plays" with his prey after injuring or killing it, is being cruel. In reality, the behaviour is most likely a displacement due to the excitement and anxiety of the hunt. During the hunt the cat must deal with the fear of getting injured himself in the process.'
>
> Pam Johnson-Bennett, *Think Like a Cat*

While it may be unpleasant to see a dead animal brought into the home, don't punish the cat. He is simply following his natural instincts and trying to share his resources with his human family. If the behaviour is annoying, it's best to dispose of the animal quietly when your cat isn't looking.

There are steps you can take to limit your cat's hunting success and with it the number of carcasses on your kitchen floor:

- Use a bell on his collar to alert wildlife of his approach.

- Be cautious when positioning bird feeders; avoid placing them low to the ground.

- Avoid letting your cat out at night and early morning when prey is active.

- Redirect his hunting energy through play using toys that mimic prey.

- Provide an alternative food source such as puzzle feeders or interactive feeding toys to satisfy his hunting instincts.

- Use scent deterrents like citrus, lavender or eucalyptus in areas where you don't want your cat to go.

If you think that having to secretly bin the occasional dead bird or mouse is inconvenient, call to mind the compromise that your cat makes every day to live with you. In her book, *The Lion in the Living Room*, Abigail Tucker sums this sacrifice up perfectly. House cats 'relinquish their nocturnal

119

lifestyle to match their owner's circadian rhythms. They make do with a territory that's one ten-thousandth the size of some of their feral brethren's. They renounce mating. And, for the most part, they give up killing, the pastime that defines every fibre of the feline being.'

If you've ever wondered why your cat dumps her toys in the water bowl or on your pillow, this uncharacteristically slovenly act of mischief can also be explained by your cat's hunting instinct. Cats view their toys as prey and instinctively stash them away in a secure area. In the absence of a nest, the water and food bowls become their designated 'territory' and the toys are often placed there. Also, cats may enjoy the texture of wet toys or playing with water, making the bowl a fun and interactive plaything.

As for the wet toys on your pillow, this may be due to your cat's hunting instinct conflicting with the fact that she is already well-fed by you. The surplus 'prey' may be seen as a gift or an offering and placing it on your pillow may be a sign of trust or a way of asking you to take care of it.

So next time your cat does this, remember to provide her with a fresh bowl of water and perhaps appreciate the complex instincts and behaviours that make cats such fascinating pets.

THERE'S A STORM
BREWING

THROUGHOUT HISTORY, CATS AND OTHER
ANIMALS HAVE BEEN BOTH REVERED AND FEARED
FOR THEIR SUPPOSED ABILITY TO PREDICT NATURAL
DISASTERS LIKE STORMS, EARTHQUAKES
AND VOLCANIC ERUPTIONS.

More recently, cats have also gained attention for their ability to detect illness in humans. However, this sixth sense has often been shrouded in mystery and has caused both admiration and persecution towards cats.

Modern seismographs have helped us better understand how cats can predict natural disasters such as earthquakes. These instruments are capable of detecting foreshocks, which are small tremors that gradually intensify and become more frequent prior to a larger earthquake. Cats are highly attuned to vibrations, and they likely sense these foreshocks through their feet and whiskers. As the vibrations become stronger and more frequent, cats may become agitated, like how we sense impending danger in horror films. Scientists hope to develop a system based on this understanding to offer limited early warnings of natural disasters.

> 'If we all learned cat-speak, we would often find they are saying, "You stupid human, I am trying to tell you something important right now!"'
>
> Leah Broadby

There are also simpler mechanisms at work: a cat's inner ear may detect the sudden fall in atmospheric pressure and his superior hearing means he will detect the rumble of a thunderstorm before you do. The hearing of a cat for sounds of 70 dB SPL ranges from 48 Hz to 85 kHz, which is one of the broadest among mammals. Average human hearing is in the range of 20 Hz to 20 kHz, which means that we ought to be able to hear a low rumble better than our feline friends, but modern humans are less attuned to their environment than cats, who instinctively pay more attention to the smells, sounds and sights around them.

Cats possess an acute sense of smell that enables them to detect the release of chemicals into the air that precede a volcanic eruption. Similarly, when a storm is approaching, cats may rely on their olfactory and gustatory senses in addition to their sensitivity to electromagnetism. The presence of electrical activity during a storm generates sensations that cats can detect through their fur and whiskers. Some cats may rub their ears before a storm, possibly indicating that changes in air pressure are affecting their sensitive inner ear. Even humans have a limited ability to smell an approaching storm, as the air carries the scent of ozone down from higher altitudes. Ozone has the chemical symbol O_3 because each molecule of ozone has one more oxygen atom than regular oxygen (O_2), which makes it smells zingy and fresh.

'I believe cats to be spirits come to earth. A cat, I am sure, could walk on a cloud without coming through.'

Jules Verne

I'M EIGHTY-SIX
YOU KNOW

IN HER BOOK *MODERN CAT HEALTH*, DR SARAH
BROWN MENTIONS SOME OF THE MANY CHANGES
THAT OLD AGE CAN BRING A CAT, BOTH PHYSICAL
AND BEHAVIOURAL. 'PHYSICALLY THEY MAY BEGIN
TO SUFFER FROM DENTAL DECAY, FAILING EYESIGHT
AND HEARING, STIFFNESS IN THE JOINTS AND OTHER
CLASSIC "OLD AGE" PROBLEMS ... BEHAVIOURALLY,
ELDERLY CATS MAY BECOME MORE AFFECTIONATE
TOWARD THEIR OWNERS OR QUITE THE OPPOSITE.'

Scientists now use Epigenetics – the investigation of modifications in gene expression that result in changes in organisms – to reach a more precise understanding of how animals age compared to humans. Research indicates that cats and dogs age quickly in the first two years of their lives, but this decelerates as they grow older.

The formula for determining their corresponding age is relatively straightforward: the first two years of a cat's life are comparable to 24 human years, and each subsequent year is equivalent to four human years. As an illustration, a 13-year-old cat would be equal to a 68-year-old person.

Cats are 'senior' once they reach 11 years old and their needs usually change from this age. Here are some useful tips to keep your 11+ cat happy and healthy:

DENTAL HEALTH: Taking care of your cat's teeth and gums is crucial for his dental health. The accumulation of tartar in cats can lead to numerous adverse effects.

DIET: Proper nutrition from an early age is crucial for ensuring a long and healthy life, but it becomes increasingly vital during a cat's later years. Senior cat food generally contains high-quality protein but with fewer calories to help them maintain an ideal weight, despite an increase in activity levels. Some senior cat foods contain additional ingredients, such as vitamin E, that can enhance the immune system and aid joint health. It is advisable to consult with your veterinarian regarding your cat's individual dietary needs and whether switching to senior food is necessary.

EXERCISE: Although your cat may be aging, he still needs regular exercise if his health allows it. While he may not be as nimble as before, consistent exercise can help sustain muscle mass and decrease the chances of obesity.

FELINE COGNITIVE DYSFUNCTION: Feline Cognitive Dysfunction (FCD), which refers to the decline in cognitive ability, is estimated to affect over 55% of cats aged between 11 to 15 years and more than 80% of cats aged between 16 to 20 years. This can have an adverse impact on memory, learning capacity, and senses such as sight and hearing, which can manifest in various ways as it influences a broad range of abilities. If you observe any of these symptoms in your cat, such as eliminating outside of the litter box near sleeping or eating areas, difficulty recognizing familiar people and pets, fixed staring, aimless wandering, inability to navigate around obstacles with no apparent physical cause, reduced appetite or personal grooming, reduced activity and motivation, increased irritability and anxiety, excessive vocalization, disrupted sleep (e.g. sleeping more during the day and being restless and vocal at night), it is recommended that you consult with your veterinarian regarding a possible FCD diagnosis.

OBESITY: As cats age, they often experience a decrease in energy expenditure, which may result in weight gain and

loss of muscle mass. However, it is crucial to ensure that your cat maintains a healthy weight. Obesity can cause excessive pressure on the joints and lead to various health issues, like humans.

TEMPERATURE CONTROL: Due to alterations in his metabolism, an older cat is generally more susceptible to drastic temperature fluctuations. Like older humans, he has a reduced ability to thermoregulate, particularly if his mobility is limited and makes it difficult for him to groom himself.

If you would like to learn more about how to take care of your senior cat, you can check out *Complete Care for Your Aging Cat* by Amy Shojai, a well-known animal behaviour consultant. This book contains reassuring accounts of successful senior cats and comprehensive cat reference material derived from interviews with over 100 veterinary experts.

'That's the trouble with living things. Don't last very long. Kittens one day, old cats the next. And then just memories. And the memories fade and blend and smudge together.'

Neil Gaiman

NOTES

Use the space below to note any observations you've made about your cat's behaviour.